Why Smart People Do Stupid Things

Why Smart People Do Stupid Things

Gene F. Ostrom, Ph. D.

Writer's Showcase

San Jose New York Lincoln Shanghai

Why Smart People Do Stupid Things

Writer's Showcase
an imprint of iUniverse.com, Inc.

For information address:
iUniverse.com, Inc.
5220 S 16th, Ste. 200
Lincoln, NE 68512
www.iuniverse.com

ISBN: 0-595-18798-6

Printed in the United States of America

This book is dedicated to my wife of forty-six years, Sara Willingham Ostrom. Among the many ways she has contributed to my life, has been her continuing contribution to my understanding of people and the expansion of my knowledge about children's needs. She is a humanist. Her professional career as a speech therapist and educator was marked by an unparalleled dedication to the best interests of children. She was an innovator in the application of communication skills in public school settings. She knew how children should be taught language and she knew that the social context in which language was expressed was paramount. The spoken language had to be clear, logical, relevant and appropriate to the interpersonal setting in which it occurred. Many thousands of children have benefitted from her expertise and devotion to them.

In writing this book, I have benefitted from her steadfast encouragement and direct assistance in editing and proof reading. I have been blessed.

Contents

Introduction

In recent years, a great deal has been said and written about optimizing human performance. There have been many successful motivational, inspirational, and efficiency experts telling the world how to gain both personal and career successes and how to achieve peak performances in the things they undertake. This is well and good. However, it is equally important not to overlook the negative side of peoples' behavior. The famous psychoanalyst Carl G. Jung[1] said it best as he described the essential need for man to address his "dark side" as well as his good side. He very much emphasized the importance for man to gain self-knowledge. Knowing strengths, capacities, and potentials is of vital significance in man's fulfilling his goals. His ability to gain self-understanding must include discernment of the pitfalls within his psychological makeup.

Carl G. Jung (1875-1961) was one of the famous triumvirate in the psychoanalytic movement. The other two were the founder, Sigmund Freud, and colleague Alfred Adler.

Though there was considerable mutual respect between Jung and the elder Freud, Jung always held reservations about the "Professor." These were based on deep dismay at Freud's personal life, Freud's insistence on the primacy of the sex drive, and most of all of Freud's dogmatism. Jung was dedicated to science which demanded that everything was subject to

---

[1] Rohrback, Elizabeth C. [Ed.] Jung's Contribution to Our Time: The Collected Papers of Eleanor Bertine (New York: G. P. Putnam's Sons, 1967).

questioning and testing. Any effort to restrain an individual from independent thinking was abhorrent to him.

During the years of my college education in the field of psychology (ending with graduation in 1962), there had been a great deal of emphasis upon behaviorism. Much attention had been given to the experimental (empirical) study of behavior with a reductionist bias. The learning process was tested over and over using mice as the preferred subjects. Leaders of the field at that time were Clark Hull and B. F. Skinner. Hull, a former engineer turned psychologist, developed an intricate symbolic system to describe experimental findings, a system approaching the precision of mathematics. Skinner was noted for *operant conditioning* wherein the subject (mostly mice and pigeons) initiated the responses which were subsequently shaped by learning (his name is associated with the "Skinner box," a device for establishing and measuring conditioning). Such elementary letter symbols as the following were employed: S=subject, R=response, O=organism. The theoretical field divided itself into those who were for S-R learning and those advocating S-O-R. The former, in essence, left the mind out of the learning equation. To the behaviorist all that was necessary was to identify the stimulus and the associated response. The "O" was referred to as "the black box." The inference was that we could never know with scientific certitude what went on inside that box otherwise known as the brain.

Since Carl Jung was so far removed from this sort of conceptualization, he was usually ridiculed by my professors as dealing with voodoo rather than science. Jung was for many years cast in the background of those contributing to the understanding of human behavior. That has changed considerably in the last half of this century. Jung, writing in 1957, believed that man had done a very poor job of gaining self-knowledge. He attributed the failure, in part, to our regarding the psyche (the mind) as emanating from the mechanical functions of the brain and it's having no substantive effect on behavior. This notion was consistent with the materialistic and mechanical view of science that began with Sir Isaac Newton. At the same time, as noted above, too many regarded the psyche as being beyond man's ability to comprehend it's nature. The workings of the mind were thought to be ethereal and mysterious, not conducive to scientific investigation.

Jung also recognized that man was terrorized by the thought of facing his inner core of being. Man was split in his psychic world between the conscious and unconscious. An insurmountable barrier stood between the two so that an integration could not take place. Why? Man's consciousness grew out of the unconscious both phylogenetically and ontogenically. Instincts served to protect our species and ourselves from all assaults against the integrity of the organism. Preservation and comfort was the goal. As consciousness emerged, so did problems for the mind to contend with. The time of pre-consciousness and the period of early childhood were like paradise. There is a vestige of longing for this problem free, simple, smooth, and certain existence. Unfortunately for such desires, reality will have it's way. The instinctual life though wrapped in shadows still drives us to turn away from problems and seek the calming effects of certitude. A fully free and creative conscious life is thus impeded.

Acceptance of the Jungian approach was sparked by Einstein's publication of his general theory of relativity in 1915. That launched the physical sciences on a new course, away from the closed-system of Newtonian theorizing to open-systems characterized by quantum theory. This shift in cognitive approach had been long anticipated by Carl Jung. There had been no area that might have relevance to man's psychological condition which Jung didn't give his considered attention. He was the embodiment of the open minded man. It was this changing *Zeitgeist* that helped increasing numbers of people to explore Jung's thinking.

Jung believed that in everything we undertake in life there are driving forces of opposites. He refers to them as the *shadow side* of our psyche which essentially means the unconscious side. We must learn to pay attention to both our manifest and hidden natures even though it is a difficult challenge. Failure to do so accounts for much of our stupid failures.

Common wisdom supports Jung's thesis when we speak of learning from our mistakes.

We still hear the plaintive cry of "why?" when intelligent, well educated people—especially those of high personal achievement—engage in stupid behaviors. This phenomena doesn't apply only to individuals. We see various groups making dumb decisions. Among them are churches, businesses, political parties, legislative bodies, the judiciary, and nations. We commonly discover within the varying specialties of business, industry, and science the commission of serious errors. From food processing, automobile manufacturing, cigarette marketing, and genetic engineering, we see faulty decisions being made that should have either been foreseen or tested prior to their implementation.

Some have recognized that being forewarned is to half-way achieve success. Open mindedness allows us to weigh a broader array of evidence before making critical decisions. Sensitivity to our own neurotically driven motives, our greed, conceit, and arrogance can reduce foolish moves. After the sinking of the Titanic, the Titanic Society was formed. Its purpose was to call attention to the fact that "the unsinkable ship" sank despite the claims of owners and the manufacturer. The marvels of the technological revolution should not blind us to the fact that bright, educated human beings are still subject to making extravagant claims and stupid mistakes. Man does not have absolute control.

What has brought me to write about this topic? I bring to the subject nearly a lifetime of distilled experience. When fifteen or sixteen years old, while poking around a second-hand book store, I came across a book titled: *Adult Infantilism In the United States*.[2] It opened my adolescent mind to the real world of adulthood. Mature people's behavior often bordered on the infantile. Subsequently, I was intrigued as a high school

---

[2] Collins, Joseph. Adult Infantilism in the United States [or prefaced by: A Doctor Looks at] (Publisher unknown, copywrite circa. 1930).

student when I read Sigmund Freud's essay on the *Psychopathology of Everyday Life.*[3] It, too, showed frailty in the human mind.

Several reasons were probably behind my desire to devalue the thinking of adults.

First was the feeling that many adults (my parents not among them) were either condescending to me or out-right rude. Second was probably my adolescent way of rebelling. Third was my own insecurities about conducting my life in a rational manner.

I had plenty of reasons for doubting my ability to do so.

After reaching adulthood, I was not immune, of course, to making stupid errors. There is one that I can recall very clearly that illustrates at least two points. One is the phenomenon of repression and its effects on conscious memory. Point two relates to how it is that people can exhibit amnesia when it serves them well to do so. I had purchased a two-year-old 1981 Ford Econovan to use as a utility vehicle. I had driven it to work one day anticipating a visit to a building supply store before returning home. After eating lunch, I thought there was enough time to visit the store prior to returning to the job. I was still unfamiliar with driving such a cumbersome vehicle as the van was to me. Consequently, I cautiously backed the van into an open space between two other cars. Each of those also faced outwardly toward the exit route. When departing from the store, I was in a hurry and I remember extending my arm upward to glance at my watch. I got into the van, started the engine, and pulled out towards my right. The van, having had abusive use by the previous owner, broadcast excessive noises from the engine and a good number of rattles from the truck body. What then occurred, what I was aware of, and what I later could reconstruct from memory were very different. Besides the noise of the vehicle, I was marginally conscious of hearing something else. What I heard was the right side of the van scraping the left front fender and head

---

3 Freud, Sigmund. "Psychology of Everyday Life" as contained in Brill, A. A. [Ed.] The Basic Writings of Sigmund Freud (New York: The Modern Library, 1938).

xvi • *Why Smart People Do Stupid Things*

light of the car parked to my right. Upon reflection days later, it came to me that my awareness at that moment consisted of "I may have bumped the car next to me. If I had, there was probably no damage. I've got to get back to work to avoid being late." At the moment of the accident, these thoughts went through my mind in a flash and they were then gone, out of mind.

At work, about a half hour to three quarters of an hour later, I received a telephone call from a county police officer asking if I drove such and such a vehicle. I unhesitatingly replied "yes." He then went on to give a few details about a collision in the building supply's parking lot. I was astonished because at that moment I had no memory of what had transpired. A witness' report included the detail of my looking at the wrist watch upon exiting the store. That I remembered. I attributed my failure to remember as being the result of lack of awareness that it had occurred at all. I believed the various noises from my van kept me from detecting the noises from the crash. The fact of the matter was that I had done an excellent job on myself of *repressing* the event. If I had taken a lie detector test, I'm sure I would have passed it with respect to not knowing that the collision happened. In spite of the over zealous police officer who charged me (and in his mind had me convicted) with leaving the scene of an accident, I was acquitted by the judge. Whether or not the judge believed me I don't know. He was favorably impressed by the fact that I made prompt restitution to the car owner. If my memory now serves me right, if convicted I could have lost my drivers license, been fined a thousand dollars, and spent a year in jail.

This anecdote about my stupidity made it clear to me what many a criminal attorney has said about his client. They declare their innocence and behave as though they were true. I believe amnesia plays a part but over a lengthy trial some awareness is most likely to break through. I think O. J. Simpson displayed some amnesia following the murders of Nicole and Ron.

This book is arranged so as to address certain major questions in a logical sequence. It begins in Chapter I with an exploration of the idea of smartness. How do we normally think of it? What is it, really, according to the best of scientific research? The opposite issue is then addressed in Chapter II. What is meant by the expression "being stupid?" The answer is far from simple. Chapter III considers the age-old question of freewill. Do we really choose? This is followed in Chapter IV by a look at samples from everyday life that we generally have regarded as being stupid. In Chapter V, the oftentimes puzzling question of why is there so much stupidity is examined. Chapter VI looks at additional factors explaining stupidity. Chapter VII searches for possible solutions for individuals and society The last chapter brings me to a conclusion.

So, why do smart people do stupid things?

CHAPTER I

What Is Smartness and How Do We Determine It?

Definitions

From the Dictionary

Webster's dictionary[4] contains the following relevant definition of "smart." It is "having or showing *quick* intelligence or *ready* mental capability [*ital ics* mine]." And what of intelligence? The first defining entry is "capacity for learning, reasoning, understanding, and similar forms of mental activity; aptitude in grasping truths, relationships, facts, meanings, etc. The second entry is "manifestation of a *high* mental capacity….[*Italics* mine]" The dictionary has captured accurately how we ordinarily regard use of the words smartness and intelligence.

---

[4] Webster's New Universal Unabridged Dictionary. (New York: Barnes & Noble Books, 1996).

Casual Impressions

In our casual contacts with people, we judge their smartness by things they say, how they say it, how they approach and solve everyday problems, and their conduct in general. We would apply as standards for making such judgments what we know and expect of ourselves and our accumulated, cultural knowledge of what constitutes intelligence.

People's casual judgments about others' capacity for smart behavior is far from accurate (the true accuracy being measured by some objective means). It is not infrequent that two observers of the same act regard it as being smart from one's perspective and stupid from the other's. As casual judgments they are more like guesses and they are subjective in nature. The evaluation reflects our personal ideas. Parents, particularly those of younger children, are often out of sync in assessing their child's intelligence against neighbor's and teacher's opinions. As a professional psychologist (whose job it often was to objectively measure individual intelligence), I frequently was at a loss in judging a client's intellectual ability by informal observation. I have, in fact, been shocked when seeing the discrepancy between the results of testing and my prior estimate.

It does not always matter a great deal in daily life whether we are accurate or not in our perception of the functional intelligence of those who interact with us. So long as people live up to normal standards in performing their various formal roles, we don't question their smartness. For example, the librarian follows the proper procedures in checking out books. She can give you accurate directions on where to find what you are looking for. She could instruct you on how to use the library's computer to search the index of book listings. Her intellectual level could vary from low average to genius. Who cares? The same thing can be said of your barber, hairdresser, mail carrier, etc.

On the other hand, in ordinary life there are times when it is important to have a ready and accurate perception of how someone is functioning intellectually. It would be a question of whether or not they have "good enough" intelligence to deal with a particular situation. A simple example would be asking directions from someone in a strange city. Another would be to depend on a stranger to call for help in the event of an accident. Would the person have the ability to locate a nearby telephone and dial 911? Supposing you are in a dispute with someone. Perhaps it has to do with receiving what you judge to be incorrect change from the bank teller or a fender-bender accident. The effects of emotional reactions aside, your discussion (or argument) must be geared to the intellectual level of the disputant. People have been killed in similar situations for failure to appreciate intellectual differences.

Intelligence becomes an issue more frequently with respect to performance in formal roles. In this case there is considerable confounding between intelligence, knowledge, and various personality variables. Does the accountant handle your tax problem correctly? No. You're in a jam. It may be because he's ignorant, lazy, emotionally unstable, or not quite smart enough. When you selected him to work for you, such variables should have been assessed. The same applies in choosing anyone to provide you with a service. This is true whether it is an auto mechanic, doctor, or politician.

As mentioned above, it is no easy task to make an accurate assessment on how well someone is functioning intellectually. It is exceedingly important, however, in your *meaningful* contacts with other people, that you seriously question in your own mind whether the person has enough smarts. How might you do this?

In response to this question, you must give attention to yourself. Firstly, with respect to your own utterances, you must be tuned into the clarity and sincerity of what and how you say things. The sort of self-monitoring that is required is not easy to do because it is not our typical way speaking. The often stated question when one talks of "am I making myself clear?" is an effective technique to further insure that you will achieve understanding. However, it is much better if the question is obviated by assessing the degree of clarity yourself without asking. Listening to yourself while talking calls for a splitting of consciousness. It is like going along on parallel paths where there is no interference between the two processes. The famous psychiatrist, Theodor Reik[5], used the expression "listening with a third ear." His meaning was to perfect the ability to listen to himself as well as to the patient for unconscious processes which can mean disguised messages and associated feelings. A related process should be done as you speak, listening to yourself at a more superficial level for such things as voice quality, clearness, and feeling tone.

Listening with a third ear directed toward yourself is important because you are better able to insure that there will be effective communication. To insure understanding, you will want to hear and observe from your listener what you perceive to be accurate feedback. That is more likely to happen if your message was conveyed unambiguously. You may assess your listener's smartness to some extent by his holding up his end of the communication process.

You will be looking for coherent, relevant, and meaningful speech accompanied by congruent body language. Coherent means that words are put together in proper syntax. Relevant is staying on the point, addressing the subject at hand. Whether someone can do this or not will depend upon the breadth and preciseness of his fund of information and his mental status. The information may be general or very specific as in a technical field. Meaningful is simply that, altogether, sense can be made of it. Congruence in body language is important to be assured that mixed messages aren't being conveyed. Non-verbal communication offers a glimpse into feelings.

You would, of course, rely on previous experience with an individual as well as personal references to estimate how well the person functions intellectually. One's past is usually the best predictor of present and future capability.

---

5 Reik, Theodore. The Search Within: The Inner Experiences of a Psychoanalyst (New York: Grove Press, Inc., 1956).

Smartness has been studied and subjected to scientific ways of measurement. One would think that Webster, as cited above, covered it all with regard to providing an adequate definition. This is far from being true. Webster's words are abstractions not easily reduced to their referents in observable behaviors. The issue is far from being resolved today. It remains an important personal, educational, and social issue.

The Intelligence Quotient

To grasp the nature of the problem, it is helpful to review briefly the history pertaining to the definition and measurement of intelligence. The launching point came in 1904 when the French Minister of Public Instruction approached the psychologist Alfred Binet to assist in the development of a means of classifying children in terms of their potential for learning. At that time there was an influx of children from rural France and the French provinces into urban areas. Most of these migrants were ill prepared to undertake the formal curriculum of the urban public schools. Binet, in partnership with Theodore Simon, devised a scale in 1905 to differentiate children between the ages of three and eleven according to mental function. The test underwent several revisions within six years of the original and the 1911 scale was extended to adults. In America, Lewis Terman of Stanford University was responsible for making a major revision of the Binet-Simon scales and published the Stanford-Binet test in 1916. It was the first test to introduce the idea of an intelligence quotient (IQ).

The 1905 Binet-Simon scale was made up of items that Binet thought reflected intelligence. The items focused primarily on tests of judgment, comprehension, and reasoning (some being arithmetical in nature). These depended upon verbal skills. There were other items measuring sensory and perceptual abilities as well. Interestingly, all such items remain the backbone of intelligence testing to this day.

Items were selected empirically by establishing which ones could be passed by normal children of a particular age. Those taking the test were then assigned a mental age according to the level of performance obtained.

Terman's introduction of the IQ was useful because it took chronological age into account as well. The IQ equaled mental age divided by chronological age times one hundred (IQ=MA/CA X 100 as in MA of 10 and a CA of 10, times 100 equals 100; deemed to be an average IQ).

There was the general belief that the IQ remained constant throughout life. For this to occur in children, they would have to score consistently with the mental age norm for each advancing chronological year (e.g. the twelve year old who reaches the age of thirteen must achieve an MA score of 13 to remain average). This constancy of IQ was commonly accounted for as the result of the heritability of intelligence. This issue was the nature versus nurture debate. Much of the early supporting evidence regarding genetics was of questionable scientific value.

The basis of establishing what was normal for a given age was to test a large random sample of children (Terman used 1000 children in his original 1916 sample). In general, an item was assigned to a particular mental age when fifty percent of those passing it were of that chronological age (statistical procedures were refined in further revisions and adult scales were presumed to max out at age sixteen).

Another presumption to go along with the fixedness of the IQ is the concept of a single measure of intellectual functioning—the IQ score was it. Then and later there was some dispute over this idea of general intelligence ("g" factor). This will be elaborated on shortly.

There are two underlying statistical notions about intellectual measurements (the general field of psychometrics). One is that of reliability and the other is validity. The significance of these two concepts cannot be overestimated.

Reliability is a matter of consistency. Does the test yield essentially the same result each time it is administered? (By test we mean a number of items contributing to a single score of a particular variable such as intelligence). One would not use a flexible rubber yardstick to take linear measurements. You likely would get different results each time it is used. Commonly, reliability can be assessed either by testing on different occasions and comparing results or it can be done by the split/half technique. The latter is the procedure of comparing the answers to odd numbered questions against those of even ones.

Reliability is expressed as a correlation where one variable is related to another. When there is no relationship (the two variables are in effect independent of one another), the reliability is indicated by a "0." A plus one (+1) reliability reflects perfect concordance in which both scores move equally in the same direction. A reliability measure of minus one (-1) shows that as one score gets higher the other gets lower in the same incremental stages. A perfect correlation is rare. In testing, two items or tests showing a correlation of eight/tenths (+or-.8) is considered a very strong relationship.

The second important testing variable is that of validity. Validity is whether or not the test measures what it is purported to measure. Does the intelligence test *consistently* identify (and thus discriminate) the variable defined as intelligence? Note the italicized word "consistently." For the test to be valid it must also be reliable. You can have a reliable test that is not valid. For example, a cloth tape measure commonly used in sewing will measure the same as a yard stick. If the tape measure should go through a washing and shrink, it will still consistently measure off inches but it is no longer in agreement with the yardstick. An inch on one ceases to be the same as an inch on the other (it is as though the definition of "inch" changes). The shrunken tape remains reliable; though reduced in length, it will measure the same each time it is used. But, in its changed condition, it is no longer valid.

Validity is where most of our testing goes wrong. It depends on a definition and the linking of the definition to the test results. The means for doing this is contained in the definition itself. Now this can be done and it has been done in a rather loose fashion. For example, validation has been related to grades in school. It is assumed that getting good grades are a reflection of good intelligence. Therefore, test results should discriminate between low and high achievers in school. Similarly, (and more loosely) validation has been related to the judgments by psychiatrists as to whether the children are or are not intelligent. Thus, intelligence test scores should bear out the accuracy of the psychiatrist's judgments.

A further validation procedure for revised and new intelligence tests was to compare them with performances on old, traditional tests.

The above examples of validation state in effect that the definition of intelligence is based on school performance, psychiatrists' opinions, and traditional tests. For a good while, this was regarded as satisfactory. However, test makers soon realized that school grades typically depended on the subjective assessment by teachers, that psychiatrists' notions of intelligence varied widely among themselves, and that the validity of one test rested on the questionable validity of another .

The direction that test designers followed from the time of Alfred Binet was to ask questions and formulate tasks to be performed that in the test maker's minds constituted intelligent behavior. They included, as mentioned above, test items in the areas of judgment, comprehension, reasoning, sensory perception, and motor skills. J. P. Guilford[6] cites the famous experimental psychologist, E. G. Boring, as saying in 1923 that "…intelligence as a measurable capacity must at the start be defined as the capacity to do well in an intelligence test." The common short version of this quote is that "intelligence is what intelligence tests measure." It was thought that Boring was joking but, in fact, he was not. And he was right.

The earlier examples, in effect, defined intelligence as teachers' and psychiatrists' judgments. Establishing the criteria for validity (thus the definition) of intelligence on the content of the test itself introduced more objectivity.

Validating a test is a matter of seeing whether it is a good predictor of what we would regard as intelligent behavior. Typically, the test score such as the IQ is a lumping together of responses to questions we believe

---

[6] Guilford, J. P. The Nature of Human Intelligence (New York: McGraw-Hill Book Company, 1967). P. 13.

indicate good judgment, reasoning skills, mathematical competence, knowledge of vocabulary, accomplishing perceptual-motor tasks, etc. The IQ should then predict future behaviors in terms of success or failure wherein functions involving the aforementioned judgment, reasoning skills, mathematical competence and so on occur. We could look for such in college, in careers, or in various other kinds of life experiences where "success" or "failure" based on intelligence might be assessed. Are IQ tests predictive of such things? Not very well. Not well because what makes for success in later life is a very complicated matter that includes a wealth of personality and situational factors. However, someone who tested at a high level of competence on such things as math and vocabulary, when tested later on similar content, again will do quite well.

As mentioned above, the IQ was regarded as measuring the "g" factor—general intelligence. The poor record of accuracy in prediction as just mentioned cast some doubt as to whether or not there is such a thing as general intelligence. Others stepped forward with ideas of special types of intelligence. They devised measures of a number of factors they believed constituted various kinds of intelligent behaviors. This approach led to greater precision in accuracy of prediction.

Before elaborating on new developments in the definition and measurement of intelligence, something must be said about the problems that have occurred concerning the use of the IQ.

Reik[7] in 1956 wrote with some abhorrence about the abuse of the IQ. He cited numerous geniuses of history from scientists to composers who probably would have obtained only mediocre scores on IQ tests if available in their day. Reik was saying, in effect, that the IQ was a very unreliable predictor of later success in life. I remember clearly when a teenager my mother saying that "C" students had more success after leaving school

---

[7] *Op Cite.* Reik.

than did "A" students. She gave me a marvelous rationalization for "just getting by" in school. There was, however, some truth to her comment.

Big problems occurred in employing the IQ concept because of earlier mentioned assumptions. The first was that the IQ was a measure of general intelligence. The second was that it remained essentially constant throughout one's life. The third was that the IQ was determined primarily by genetics. I will dispense with these assumptions at this time by simply saying they are dead wrong.

Among the worst offenders in using the IQ were educators. A test was given and the reported result was that the child's IQ "is" (a specific number). It translates that the child *is* a number. It was not stated that the child on this particular occasion, with this examiner, and this test performed as follows.... Children were identified essentially by an IQ number. They were labeled as "being a 90," "a 100," "a 120," etc. Certain ranges of scores were labeled by definition and sometimes euphemistically by such terms as "idiot," "feeble-minded," "borderline," "dull," "slow," and, of course, "superior," and "genius." The latter two may have been lumped together by their school chums as "nurds." The children, thus labeled, were perceived by teachers and other school personnel as fitting within one or another of these categories. Decisions were made as to what classes they were assigned to, thus who they would associate with, and whether they would go on to college. The IQ number assigned to a particular child frequently was based on a single test, administered in elementary school, (oftentimes by way of an unreliable group, machine-scorable, paper-and-pencil test). It followed the student through the rest of his schooling. There are innumerable extraneous factors that can affect a child's test performance. Let it be said that the odds weigh heavily against a single IQ test or even several for a particular child being reliable and valid.

A much used and key word in the world of testing is "standardized." It is the psychometrician's euphemism for "experimental." Test construction and test administration is likened to the precision of a scientifically controlled experiment under laboratory conditions. The creation of tests involves such things as selection of a group of subjects to provide normative data. The criteria for inclusion in the sample is usually based on random selection or a "stratified random sample" (random selecting among pre-defined categories of subjects). The method of establishing "norms" is regarded as a standardized procedure.

Because of the selection methods used, the sample is regarded as "representative." For example, proportionality can be taken into consideration when sampling. The various races within the sample could be in the same ratio as in the general population. So the claim could be made that the sample is representative of the entire U.S. population. Typically, however, a Black child's test scores are interpreted against the pooled sample, not against the sub-sample of Black children.

Standardized also applies to test administration. If a child's performance is to be compared to a normative group, then the relevant conditions regarding test taking should be the same. Test administration should be done in the same way under comparable conditions. Consequently, test administrators are usually given detailed instructions concerning testing and, particularly with individually administered tests, administrators must undergo lengthy training in the classroom and "in the field" under supervision. In fact, certification was often required to give, score, and interpret some tests.

One very interesting thing about psychometrics and the scientific experiment is that in the former data is usually gathered on a single occasion whereas in the latter, the scientist wouldn't dream of basing conclusions on a single observation.

The required standard testing conditions would include such things as a proper environment: a suitable desk and chair, good lighting, relative quiet, etc. The child should be ready to function at least in a manner typical for him. He should have had normal rest, not be excessively hungry or thirsty, not needing to go to the bathroom, and so on. There should be good rapport between the child and the examiner. The examiner should be able to vouch for the fact that the test situation itself doesn't create undue anxiety in the child. Test items must be presented to the child in precisely the same way as had been established as the standard way. If it's a vocabulary test, the words must be given in the correct order, and pronounced and enunciated consistently. The examiner must not vary his procedure to give special assistance or register approval or disapproval either by words or facial expression. The examiner must behave in such a manner and maintain suitable rapport without acting like an automaton.

Of course, the reality is that testing is done regardless of whether the child or the examiner is having a typically good day or a very bad one. One isn't always aware of what their mood is at a particular moment. A host of subjective factors enter into the entire enterprise from test construction, administration, scoring, interpretation, communication of the results, and their utilization. I will say no more on the topic.

Multiple Factors

In 1995, the psychologist, Daniel Goleman, authored a book by the title *Emotional Intelligence.*[8] The IQ was contrasted with EQ. His thesis was that these were independent of one another. However, if one were to try and predict the likelihood of success of an individual, both measures had to be taken into consideration. He used IQ in the traditional sense. His concept of EQ was that there are personal skills ranging from simple tact to judgment about human interactions. Without possessing the rudiments of them, having the highest IQ in the world would not lead to success. He was saying that smartness alone—smartness as we traditionally have understood it—doesn't go very far. More to the point, he was saying that the definition of smartness must include emotional and social variables.

Another psychologist, Howard Gardner, had much earlier (1983)[9] proposed a more radical departure from the traditional way of looking at

---

[8] Goleman, Daniel. Emotional Intelligence: Why It Can Matter More Than IQ (New York: Bantam Books, 1995).

[9] Gardner, Howard. Frames of Mind: The Theory of Multiple Intelligences (New York: Basic Books, 1983).

smartness. He introduced the term "multiple intelligences" which has since been referred to simply as "MI." Obviously, his position is an outright rejection of the idea of a single, general kind of intelligence. His theory is based on many years of research conducted by himself and numerous other psychologists and educators in particular. The empirical evidence is impressive.

He now postulates eight different kinds of intelligences.[10] Individuals possess some element of each but profiles vary regarding their relative strengths. Typically, only two or three stand out as being high in any particular individual's profile. The eight intelligences are as follows: (1) Linguistic. (2) Logical-mathematical. (3) Musical. (4) Bodily-kinesthetic. (5) Spatial. (6) Interpersonal. (7) Intrapersonal. (8) Naturalist. I will not go into detail describing these except to say that the first two, Linguistic and Logical-mathematical, are primarily what the traditional IQ measures consist of. Also, I note that Interpersonal and Intrapersonal relate to Goleman's concept of emotional intelligence and they have similar implications for an individual's success in life.

The idea of people having as an integral part of their being different kinds of intelligences can account for some instances where a seemingly smart person may at times appear stupid. Albert Einstein serves as a good example. His brilliance as a mathematician and physicist goes unchallenged but his judgment in interpersonal relations ranged from poor to stupid. Another example is the proverbial absent minded professor who is a whiz in dealing with his esoteric subject matter but he can't match his socks and he can't find his way around town. The very successful musician, computer specialist, and botanist can't readily gain information from reading a book and they struggle in trying to compose a letter or memo.

Part of the difficulty in judging someone's smartness in an informal or offhanded way may be due to social, ethnic, and cultural differences. The same

---

[10] Gardner, Howard. Intelligence Reframed: Multiple Intelligences for the 21st Century (New York: Basic Books, 1999).

is true with respect to formal intelligence testing. Back in the early 1960's psychologists became aware of this problem and they attempted to devise "culture-free," or "culture-fair" tests. They only achieved limited success. The degree of diversity in life experience between the test taker and the normative sample used in the construction of the test affected validity. The greater the difference: the less valid the test. The westernization of world cultures, that includes the internationalization of the English language through satellite TV and the Internet, and so on will reduce differences to the point that they will become increasingly less relevant. However, they still are of major concern in measuring intellectual functioning.

Children reared in poverty, those having a single parent, the newly immigrated in a bilingual household, for example, are still prevalent in our country. They and a variety of others having special needs cannot be assessed by traditional IQ tests. I have encountered children reared in this country as well as from third world nations who have never used a pencil. They had never seen a telephone, much less a TV. Many urban or ghetto youngsters growing up amid drugs, violence, and all sorts of crime are in a vastly different world than the majority of the nation's children. They must learn to get along in their environment which is to say "survive." The kind of smartness required to do this is unlike that required in other environments. The type of smartness they develop there doesn't serve them well in the classroom. If a middle class Caucasian child were transplanted into a poverty environment, he might not have the smarts to survive for long.

Measurement

Cultural Determinants

Are we talking about a different kind of intelligence? Just maybe we are. Some psychologists have recently conceptualized intelligence as being situational rather than being in people's heads. There is something to be said for the idea. Even a computer specialist functions as he does because of accommodating to the specific work place he is in. Engineers graduating from college will tell you that their education doesn't begin until they are on the job. So much of what matters to us lies outside of us. A focus primarily upon what is in our minds and our internal organs can lead us astray. New technologies and gadgets are filling our phenomenal world and changing our very nature.

Several decades ago when my children were teenagers there was much public controversy about the generation gap. It was in the early seventies and problems in communication were real. A generation is defined by the typical genealogist as being from twenty to twenty-five years. My children informed my wife and me that the generational differences had narrowed to four or five years. They declared that as senior high students they couldn't fathom what the sixth and seventh graders were saying or doing. I think they were right and I still think that is the way it is.

One thing I notice a great deal is a change in what I would regard as *attention span*. This is an impression and not based upon experimental testing. It seems that those of my generation could focus with interest on a slow paced story. Even a TV commercial got their eye when it was directly factual, descriptive, and repetitive. Commercials today are anything but that. They are indirect, visual rather than verbal, and flash by with no logical transition from one image to another. The so-called thirty second spot commercial has, I believe, been reduced to half that time. News stories are now given in snippets rather than as a cohesive whole. These changes in the way stimuli reach our senses affect perception and they in turn affect our cognition—the way we reason, solve problems, relate to other people. They make smartness a more complex matter.

Demonstrated Performance

Gardner's theory of multiple intelligences[11] speaks to a new type of pedagogy. I go into this in the final chapter. It also speaks of a new way to evaluate

---

[11] *Ibid.*

intelligence and academic achievement. His basic concept about measuring is captured in the phrase *performance of understanding*. The question whether a child or someone of any age has the capacity to grasp a particular concept, perform a certain task, and gain a skill can be answered if in some way or another he or they can demonstrate their comprehension and mastery. The proof must be based on a process not as a single testing occasion or a series of discrete measures. Demonstrated competence need not be achieved on a specific date or within a defined time frame. Where we are dealing with multiple intelligences, we also must deal with multiple kinds of performance. What of achievement, intellectual ability, smartness? We are more likely to recognize them if we are able to broaden our perspective—maybe seeing smartness where we least expect it.

CHAPTER *II*

What Is Being Stupid?

Looking at Outcome

Society's Ideas of Failure

All failures and mistakes are not the result of stupidity. We recognize that there are circumstances beyond human control. Accidents occur that cannot be foreseen. There are those things we call freaks of nature. Chance happenings and random events play a role in sub-atomic physics as well as in the vastness of the universe. We must conclude about some events that it just isn't anyone's fault.

Not everyone is ready to make such allowances. My mother, bless her soul, was an intelligent, generous, well meaning, and loving person but she was caught up in the guilt trap or blame game. I'm sure it came from her parents, particularly from her father, who had been a judge on the Montana State Supreme Court. He, too, was a generous and just person, but he was a man of rigid principles. He believed that people could move mountains if they put their minds to it. As I grew up, I often heard two expressions from my mother. One was "it's not my fault!" The other was the question "whose fault is it?" These were said as swiftly and invariably as a knee jerk response to many things that happened. It was as though my mother had a deep conviction that everything had a cause and if there were errors the cause had to be because of some human mischief or bad judgment. Fortunately, my mother was always ready to forgive me if I were the miscreant and not leave me with an excessive burden of guilt.

Aside from acts of God, we also know that people say and do stupid things. One way of assessing stupidity is to look at the outcome as it relates to motive or decision making. If we see a bad result, we can question what it was that led up to it. It was a bad result for the man who was quickly apprehended after robbing a bank. Police were able to move fast because the note he handed the bank teller was written on the back of an envelope. The note read "this is a hold-up, be quiet, and put all your money in the bag." The front of the envelope had the robber's name and address printed on it.

A recent news release that got national exposure was a tragic house fire that killed a family of eleven people in Delaware. The fire was caused by an adult member of the family who heated a pan of grease on the stovetop in preparation for cooking french fries. Everyone in the house was asleep at the time and the adult tending the stove also fell asleep.

Speaking of fires, it is commonplace for them to be started by a person falling asleep in bed while smoking a cigarette.

Uncountable are the number of times we see a bad result from being in a hurry or rush to get something accomplished. We are led to believe that such a mind set is the major cause of serious auto accidents. A recent news article warns us that we make it easy for someone to steal our cars when we leave the key in the ignition with the motor running while we hurry into the convenience store to purchase something like a pack of cigarettes. Some errors happen as a consequence of a sense of urgency. An example would be sending a computer printed check to the IRS that has a notation on it for the previous year. The payment will be applied to that year and not to the intended current year. Correcting the error involves a considerably complex process of filing an amended return for the earlier year (I speak from experience). The common saying "haste breeds waste" was coined for such occasions.

Often the source of our being hurried is to meet a deadline. Such is April 15 of each year for filing one's income tax return. Perhaps "deadlines" are so compelling because of the origin of the word that means strict demarcation of a time when something has to be done. Evans[12] writes that the sense of finality derives from the experience of Civil War prisoners at Andersonville, Georgia. If a prisoner were to cross a line some distance beyond the camp's periphery they were shot dead. Henceforth, when we think of deadlines we should realize that in all likelihood we won't be executed if we are a little late.

Speaking of common sayings or aphorisms, there are a wealth of them expressing folk wisdom. My parents' conversation was replete with aphorisms. For a good deal of my youth, I was at a loss as to what they were talking about because of my deficiency in abstract reasoning. Many of the sayings were cautionary in nature. What about "a stitch in time saves nine?" Literally, best take care of a problem at the beginning before it later becomes more difficult to correct. It is not smart to ignore reality.

I heard that "curiosity killed the cat," but contrariwise, "nothing ventured nothing gained." There's a tension there. But, we know that failure to exercise reasonable caution could lead to disaster. For example, crossing one of the great deserts in the western part of our country by automobile and not checking the gas gage first, not taking extra water, and not having a spare tire and car-jack shows a stupid lack of foresight.

"All that glitters is not gold." How many times has greed led us into a bad situation? The sales pitch to purchase "penny stocks" was extremely enticing. There was the promise of great wealth soon to be realized. "In no time the prices are going to skyrocket" we were informed. Two things happened. The prices stood still or were deflated and much money disappeared through securities' fraud. Jumping on the bandwagon of investing

---

[12] Evans, Ivor H. Brewer's Dictionary of Phrase and Fable (New York: Harper & Rowe, Publishers, 1959).

in Internet common stocks has led to a lot of grief as of this date (March 2001). The value of technical stocks has plunged, some by as much as eighty percent.

"People in glass houses shouldn't throw stones." Representative Henry J. Hyde of Illinois was vociferously critical of Clinton's lack of morals. According to Hyde, Clinton's character defects disqualified him from being the President of the United States. On September 16, 1998, while the House of Representatives was focused on Clinton's lack of morals, *Salon* Internet magazine published a story about Hyde having carried on an extramarital affair for an extended period during the early 1960's. Hyde acknowledged that in all likelihood the information had been revealed by the woman's husband. Nevertheless, Hyde blamed the White House for trying to discredit him and referred to the affair as "youthful indiscretion" though he was in his forties at the time. The maxim of having a "skeleton in one's closet" is also apropos, as may be "let sleeping dogs lie."

"Do as I saith, not as I do." This saying is essentially an admonishment by the self-righteous or a transparent attempt at rationalization. It must have been on the mind of the Reverend Jesse Jackson in 1998 as he counseled President Bill Clinton regarding the Monica Lewinsky affair. It was at that very time that the 56 year-old Jackson, married and the father of five children, impregnated a female employee, Karin Stanford. She subsequently gave birth to a daughter. After twenty months the story hit the national headlines.

It was Ms. Stanford's decision not to abort the pregnancy. She obtained a DNA test to prove that Jackson was the father. She was paid $35,000 to move to Los Angeles and was promised $3,000 a month for support. When asked early on by the press if Jackson was the father, Ms. Stanford denied it. However, it was generally known in black political circles and Jackson's wife was aware of it. Following the New Year, a reporter from the "National Inquirer" offered Ms. Stanford up to a million dollars to tell her story. She refused.

Columnist Jack E. White[13] quoting Stanford wrote that there were so many former Rainbow staff members who "'hate Jesse and want to destroy him' so much they didn't need cash as an incentive to spill what they knew."

Jackson also had many political enemies on the far right because of his own liberal political stance. He was a man who was under constant public scrutiny. He was a target for numerous opponents. Here was a man who had preached to inner-city children about the threat of AIDS and unwanted pregnancy. Safe sex commonly translated to the use of condoms.

Was Jackson guilty of an immoral act? Yes. Was he also guilty of an illegal act? Yes. Even if Ms. Stanford initiated having the sexual liaison with Jackson, he, being her employer, engaged in sexual harassment. Is Jackson seeking to excuse himself when he blames the right-wing conspiracy for discrediting him? It would appear so. Do we not shake our heads in bewilderment when an intelligent, acknowledged leader risks so much for so little?

"You can't judge a book by its cover." It is certainly commonplace for members of the opposite sex who are meeting for the first time and who may enter into a courtship to be on their best behavior. There may be a concentrated effort to try and be the person you think the other would be attracted to and possibly love. This may involve intentional concealment of recognized personal faults. Such occurs to such an extent that one partner or the other may soon after marriage declare in exasperation that "you aren't the person that I thought you were when I married you!" Unfortunately, this may be an accurate observation.

So we sometimes hear that we should "strike while the iron is hot." Similarly, the maxim might be "he who hesitates is lost" or that "the early bird gets the worm." Contrariwise, we might hear also that "fools rush in where angels fear to tread." Whichever course one follows there are times when timidity leads to lost opportunities. It has been said numerous times

---

13 White, Jack E. "The End of the Rainbow," *Time*, January 29, 2001.

"if only I had bought that piece of property when I saw that it was up for sale." Years ago there was an interesting projective psychological test— what was known as an incomplete sentence test—titled "The If-Only...." It was simply twenty unfinished sentences each beginning with "If only...." and the examinee was asked to finish them based on their personal feelings or experience. The results often were very revealing. It could have been called "the regrets test."

A saying that I often heard from my parents was "monkey see, monkey do." Their remark could have been directed to me or to some other person whose actions they didn't admire. Imitation or following the leader wasn't always the wisest move. Walking out on a frozen pond just because someone else did was not an exercise in good judgment.

One may be "burning a candle at both ends." There is danger in trying to undertake too much. This may be a failing of the person who "just can't say no." Such a person exposes himself to "burn out," slip-shod work, or neglect of other responsibilities. It's not smart.

"You are known by the company you keep." "When you lie down with dogs, you get fleas." The moral here is well illustrated by a recent case where the person's trouble stemmed from his friends or associates. The Baltimore Ravens' star linebacker, Ray Lewis, took a trip to observe the year 2000 Super Bowl in New Orleans. He picked up some acquaintances in his leased stretch limousine on the trip south from Baltimore. After the game he went with these individuals and others to the Cobalt Lounge. Upon leaving the club in the early morning hours, a fracas erupted and two young men were stabbed to death. Lewis was charged with murder along with his two companions. Lewis plea bargained, conceding to an obstruction of justice charge. The two co-defendants were later acquitted. Lewis' attorney was subsequently quoted as saying "Ray had some wrong friends." There is little or no doubt that Lewis was innocent of the murder charge.

Self Castigation for Not Meeting Own Wishes or Needs

Sometimes we are our own severest critics. We find ourselves batting our heads with our fists exclaiming "why was I so stupid?" or "I could kick myself." We will fault ourselves for things no one else would ever notice. Of course, we know ourselves like no other and we develop expectations or standards we think we should live by. We may think that we made some social faux pas and then stew about it. An example being that "I went through the reception line and forgot the name of the bride's parents." It could, of course, be something more serious like losing your plane ticket or passport. You might place yourself on the bad side of your boss by missing an important business meeting. Perhaps worse yet, you might forget your wedding anniversary. I'm sure there are many really serious things you may fault yourself for as being stupid. Another category regarding outcome is one where there is pain, injury, or death.

Actions Resulting in Pain or Injury

Broadly speaking there are two categories of pain. One is psychological and the other physical. Commonly, when physical pain occurs it is likely to be accompanied by some psychological components. Whenever someone is the agent of someone else's pain it is not always wrong. There are times when certain decisions and actions must be made and some hurtful consequences are regretfully unavoidable. The clearest example of this and one we are all familiar with is when a pediatrician gives a child an injection with a needle. The mother administering bitter tasting medicine to her child wishes that it not taste bad. She genuinely feels that "this hurts me as much as you." The policeman who justifiably pulls you over for exceeding the speed limit by fifteen miles an hour and gives you a ticket is acting as an agent of the law and his personal feelings need not be at issue. Such is the case no matter how much you are distressed.

The individual who may be identified as the immediate effective cause of something hurtful may have acted with or without intent to do harm.

Intentional acts are clearly immoral. Unintentional ones may be accidental (sometimes forgivable, sometimes qualified as negligent). Also, they may be ignorant or stupid.

Some examples of causing psychic pain through stupidity range from the simple to the complex. A rather simple one might be having received a written dinner invitation with an RSVP request and ignoring it. (Worse would be accepting the invitation and not showing up). Assuming that this is not an intentional slight, we may attribute it to forgetting, carelessness, or lack of manners. Stupidity could be a global description.

Another example is not infrequent. We have all met the big mouth who in a mixed group of people expounds upon his biased opinions of Jews, Catholics, or Blacks and so on. He causes at least some of his listeners to feel uncomfortable or wounded. It's the same kind of person who will make "jokes" that are in fact religious, ethnic, or racial slurs. Clearly, these are stupid acts, often labeled as "boorish."

The number of examples can go on endlessly when one realizes that such emotional pain is usually the result of insensitivity to other people's needs or desires. The overnight or weekend house guest who offers to help with the dishes is denied the pleasure of feeling useful and expressing gratefulness when told by the hostess "not to bother: I'd rather do it myself."

All too often we pick up our newspaper and read or see on the evening TV news a story about a family dying in a house fire. It most often occurs at night while everyone is asleep. The fire inspector comes in the morning, does his investigation, and confirms the coroner's conclusion that the deaths occurred due to smoke inhalation. Few of us realize that the deadly smoke came from a burning mattress. The mattresses that Americans sleep on are death traps. By regulation, our mattresses are constructed to resist catching on fire from a smouldering cigarette. There is no standard set for mattresses' resistance to open flame. Tests show that any and all standard mattresses will ignite in from eight to thirty seconds. As they burn they emit smoke that in itself is deadly. However, many also yield toxic fumes that include cyanide in concentrations leading to instant death. England some years ago legislated standards to protect their citizens from this hazard. In the United States, our prison population is required to sleep on safe mattresses. Tough luck to the rest of the American public. They cannot even buy a safe mattress if they wanted one because manufacturers don't produce them. I write this as of March 2001. Why aren't people informed about this problem? Why hasn't the government taken action to set industry standards? Does this not seem stupid?

A U.S. government agency, the National Transportation Safety Board, has been repeatedly asked by air safety inspectors to install fire sensors and flame suppressant devices in the cargo and baggage holds of commercial aircraft. They have refused to do so on the grounds that it is not cost effective. A dollar value is placed on each human life and the total dollar loss from deaths in the Board's mind doesn't justify the cost to the airline industry. Our sense of values can suffer because of stupidity.

This past year a great deal has been discussed about highway deaths resulting from defective Firestone automobile tires. Many of the tires were standard on the popular Ford motor vehicle known as the Bronco. There is considerable dispute between Firestone and Ford as to what degree they share responsibility. The fact has been established that at least Firestone knew for nearly four years that there was a problem with the tires. They suppressed the information during which time hundreds of people were being injured and killed because of tire failures. One can argue that this is criminal behavior. If we can look into the minds of the industry's decision makers—obviously men of intelligence—would we discover criminal intent? Would we see greed clouding over sound judgement? Would we find a level of mental functioning that is at least describable as stupid?

It seems that we are increasingly reading and hearing about both children and adults who are being killed by domestic pets. Several breeds of dogs have been responsible for vicious attacks on humans. Chief among them are the pit bull, mastiff, and Doberman Pinscher. From personal experience, I can include the German shepherd. A reader may feel that I'm maligning their dearest friend by thus identifying these particular species. I'm not. I will use my run-in with a German shepherd to illustrate a point.

Some years ago a young psychiatrist neighbor invited me into his home. We both had been outside his house where his dog was pegged on a long chain. The man of the house led the way to the door and at his bidding I followed. The dog attacked me, first biting the calf of my leg causing a deep wound and then it jumped for my throat. I'm six feet two inches tall. I threw up my right arm as protection and the dog's jaws closed on the underside of my upper arm. A substantial hunk of flesh was pulled loose. The dog's master was finally able to subdue the animal. If I were a child, it's highly likely a death would have resulted. The neighbor's apologies and offer to cover my medical expenses were not sufficient to appease me. Though I didn't file a law suit, I went to various authorities to have the dog removed, all without success. I consulted the local veterinarian about the particular dog. The vet informed me that he knew the dog and he said that he had previously advised the owner to destroy the animal. Three weeks later I learned that the dog had attacked the psychiatrist's five-year-old niece in her home by biting her face. The consequence was a severe gash in the girls face and considerable psychological trauma.

The point to be made is that the animals are not to be faulted. The owners are. Curiously, in my personal illustration, it was a psychiatrist who was responsible. A person in this profession should be trained and observant regarding behaviors of all kinds. His dog was taught to be vicious. Their purpose in having the dog admittedly was to serve as a guard for the psychiatrist's wife who was often alone in their house. Owners of dogs who don't have professional dog handling training are negligent. They just as well leave a loaded gun on the coffee table in their house or on the picnic table in their yard.

To top off this tale of stupidity regarding the danger of pets, I saw recently a TV show regarding a Texas man who kept two Bengal tigers in a fenced-in area in the rear of his house. A ten year old neighbor girl got too close to the fence and one of the beasts nearly decapitated her.

She died. The owner of the tigers was not in violation of any law in having such "pets."

We can find other examples of stupidity on a societal level. Look at the problems of availability of guns to our children and of assault weapons to criminals. Look at the problems associated with the use of tobacco products. Look at problems in education and the treatment of the elderly poor and the elderly in nursing homes. If I keep on I could soon fill several pages in enumerating our inability to resolve problems through our collective stupidity. It is by outcome that we identify stupid behaviors. We also can conceive of stupidity as a mental process.

Looking at Process

Lack of Common Sense

So often we hear of "common sense." "If people would only use their common sense" has almost become a cliche. What is it? Webster defines it in the following way: "Sound practical judgment that is independent of specialized knowledge, training, or the like; normal native intelligence." As noted in Chapter I, intelligence in itself is not easy to define or to identify; hence, Webster's pronouncement is not altogether satisfying.

Practical judgment is clearly a cognitive process, one possessed by ordinary men. Ordinary men, however, don't simply *possess* common sense. It is the man's judgement along with the *situation* itself that lets us know what common sense is. The application of common sense occurs in common situations. The civil engineer has common sense along with specialized cognitive skills. The specialized skills assist him in building super highways. Common sense alone won't get him very far with that task. However, the engineer falls back on his common sense when he sees gasolene spilling to the ground from a fuel pump. He knows from practical experience that the fumes spread along the ground faster than the liquid gasolene and the fumes are much more volatile. He sees that all sources of ignition in the area are extinguished quickly. We would label as stupid behavior that in which the ordinary man in a practical situation responds inappropriately. He lacks common sense.

Common sense is like the things that our mothers told us about or warned us of when we were children. Here are a few that readily come to mind. "Don't talk while you chew." This advice was offered long before the Heimlich maneuver was discovered. "Don't go out in the rain without your overshoes." "Don't run with scissors in your hand." "Don't cross the street between parked cars." "Look at me when I talk to you!" Making eye contact when conversing *is* generally a good thing. "Show respect to your elders!" A little bit of manners and tact can smooth the way to success. There are other types of mental processes that may expose stupidity such as illogical reasoning and invalid presentation of evidence.

Contrary to Formal Logic

We speak of one area of cognition when we say such things as "I don't see the logic in that" or "it doesn't make sense to me." Intelligent people are prone to logical error as well as those less swift mentally. There are a host of examples of non-sensible events contained in old-wives tales or traditional superstitions. Of the latter, it quickly comes to mind that "one should not cross the path of a black cat." I remember as an eight-year-old riding in the passenger seat of a pick-up truck driven by a young, male adult neighbor. We were descending a narrow, winding country road at a moderate speed. Abruptly, he jammed on the brakes, nearly throwing me through the front windshield. He jumped out of the vehicle, grabbed a broken tree limb and hurled it at a black cat darting across the road. He uttered a few curses and got back in the truck. I knew that the driver wasn't an idiot but I did recognize idiocy in his behavior at that moment.

Few realize how close we are to believing and acting on the basis of superstition and magical thinking. We appear to have a built in readiness to relinquish reason when confronted by fear and anxiety. The least provocation from perceived threat or the presence of the unknown will send us into a rampage of wild imaginings.

In the middle ages well over 100,000 women were executed on the basis of being a witch. During the same period of history, we suffered the extreme cruelty of the Catholic inquisition. It is likely that over the span of a few centuries a million or more people died on the basis of being judged a heretic, among them was Saint Joan of Arc. To prove that this was not a time of unreason, such men as Tycho Brahe, Galileo, Leonardo Da Vinci, and Michelangelo lived and expressed themselves through writing and art. Some were themselves under attack from the church.

The famous Salem Witch Hunts occurred in New England in 1692. They started because of the talk of a few hysterical girls. After an approximate twelve month period, the hunts suddenly ended because the same girls began to implicate the pastor, Rev. Samuel Parris along with the wife of the Governor. Rev. Parris was the strongest advocate of the persecutions. Thirteen people were cruelly executed. Many others were in jail awaiting death when the madness ended. Nearly all of those executed were women. Most were upstanding citizens in the community and leading church members. Rebecca Nurse (born Towne) was seventy-one years of age, a grandmother, who had been generally regarded as "the essence of what a Puritan mother should be."[14] She hanged with four others on July 19, 1692.

Even now it seems very easy for people to believe in ghosts, evil spirits, and the existence of poltergeist. Note the successes of such books and movies as *Rosemary's Baby, The Exorcist, The Blair Witch Project,* and *The Sixth Sense.* Currently there is a TV program that invites volunteers to experience various haunted houses, castles, and so on. We, of course, have been faced with the UFO phenomena and alleged abductions of humans by alien beings.

---

[14] Starkey, Marion L. The Devil in Massachusetts (New York: Doubleday & Company, Inc., Anchor Books Edition, 1969). P. 78.

Most of us have responded emotionally to weird thoughts and images by having cold chills run up and down our spines. It is probably no coincidence that cold temperatures are said to be associated with the presence of a ghost or spirit.

What all this amounts to is our readiness to be thrown back on our primitive instincts. Is it any wonder that we respond with paranoia when we imagine ourselves threatened by cultural diversity, rampant liberals, or the Eastern Establishment?

We are told that "practice makes perfect." Such a remark probably falls into the category of common wisdom sayings. Unfortunately, it frequently is unwise. One thing that can occur with practice is that we may start out correctly with our repetitions but we may drift off the mark and thus rehearse errors. Another thing is that the practice may involve rote learning without there being a potential for realistic implementation. The practice may be too specific for generalizations to occur. The phenomena has been called the transfer effect and simple replications of a fact or behavior does not necessarily result in broader, meaningful applications. The teacher who sends the student to the black board, chalk in hand, to write a hundred times "I won't forget to bring in my homework" is not teaching. She is punishing. A complex motor skill such as billiards or pool is not learned by practicing. A person can spend a lifetime at the pool table knocking balls about and never become an accomplished player. He needs to learn, preferably from instruction, about technique, strategy, and temperament.

Logic in the formal sense is arguing from assertions that are accepted as being factual. There are a number of forms called syllogisms that systematically describe deductive reasoning. A common one may be represented symbolically as: All A is C; All B is A; therefore All B is C. Substituting words goes further in illustrating the process. All heros are brave; All soldiers are heros; therefore All soldiers are brave. This is perfectly logical but it doesn't have the ring of truth. It fails because the premise "all soldiers are heros" is of questionable validity. The syllogism as stated leads to a logical conclusion (they don't always because they can be misstated). However, the incorrectness of deductive reasoning generally derives from the absence of truth in one or both premises. Another example following the same syllogistic form that we have greater familiarity with is: All Democrats are leftist; All liberals are Democrats; therefore All liberals are leftist. The syllogism has correct form. The conclusion, though often affirmed in the political world, can be questioned. Are the premises correct? The correctness largely depends upon definition. Most political scientists believe that the words "leftist" and "liberal" are extremely fuzzy in their meaning. In the practical world, many cannot agree on their definitions.

Many seemingly logical arguments are not valid because of the subtle substitution of the word "all" for that of "some." One example from our recent past was the assertion in many southern states that blacks should not be allowed to vote because they were too ignorant or unintelligent to do so. Barriers were put in place to prevent blacks from voting by requiring a poll tax and a literacy test (not fairly applied or administered). The assertion implied that *all* blacks were incapable of voting. The fact was that *some* were not as some whites were not. The barriers put in place were a subterfuge to circumvent black's right to vote.

We sometimes find ourselves losing an argument because we try to apply a false analogy. The U.S. intervention in the Vietnam war was a gradual escalation of commitment to all-out combat. Granting that the reasons for our involvement were complicated, it was driven mainly by the theory of the domino effect and the analogy to the Korean War. The analogy was false on several grounds. One was the differing histories between the two countries. They were not comparable. Because of the differences, one war was winnable while the other wasn't.

Absence of Supporting Evidence

To prove a point, we often resort to citing evidence to bolster our argument. Doing so is like engaging in inductive reasoning of sorts. Chief among stupid behaviors are those resulting from jumping to conclusions.

We make decisions having insufficient evidence. We may arrive at conclusions based on guilt by association. An entire law firm may be discredited because one of the partners knowingly cheated a client. We may treat allegations as fact. Such might be the case when a politician runs for office and his opposition makes public accusations of wrong doing. No supporting evidence is presented. However, too many are prepared to believe the worst and they may follow the dictum that if it is in print or on TV it must be true. Many errors have been made following the saying "where there's smoke, there's fire." It could be steam mistaken as smoke; it might be smouldering embers and not fire; or all too often the source of the smoke is far removed from its attributed location.

A similar problem concerning insufficient evidence and jumping to conclusions is to engage in simplistic reasoning. The exclamation "Oh! The answer is simple" is nearly universally wrong. Few things in this world are simple. When we are simplistic in our approach to problems we tend to ignore the real reasons. They may be hidden and more complex but that is not to say that they aren't discoverable. The simple answer means problems continue to plague us. The laws of Newtonian physics are relatively simple and mechanistic. They fail to account for our real, dynamic, space-time world. Hundreds of years elapsed before Einstein came along and set science on a more productive path.

Men as opposed to women in general are more prone to simplistic thinking. Men's inclination is to be action oriented and narrowly focused. They are driven to *attack* problems and quickly dispense with them. Women, on the other hand, tend to seek understanding and are willing to question and reflect before accepting an answer.

In various kinds of public discourse, we are bombarded with spurious arguments. These are given in order to influence our beliefs and behaviors. Such arguments are sometimes intentionally misleading. They can be tricks of persuasion or out-and-out lies.

They may, on the other hand, result from someone being overly wedded to his own viewpoint. A person may enthusiastically cast out phony notions to bolster his position. Such people are at times motivated to save face, not wanting to be embarrassed by losing a point.

When we listened to and watched on TV the proceedings of the O. J. Simpson trial and the impeachment hearings of Bill Clinton, we had a grand opportunity to witness twisted reasoning. Every moment we spend listening to pundits on TV, we are exposed to an avalanche of bogus arguments. If we read the editorial pages of the newspapers and magazines or web pages on the Internet we are faced with the same sort of propaganda. Those wanting to influence us are oftentimes very clever in disguising their duplicity

George E. Snyder, former Maryland Senate Majority Leader, cautions us not to be a victim of "spin doctors." He refers to them also as being "spinners" or "spinmeisters." He asserts that "the citizens of the United States are constantly being used as bait or suckers to politicians' intent on misleading us with the heavy handed use of **spin techniques**....Lying, deceit and manipulation are the order of the day." Though focusing on politics as a former insider, he also zeros in on lobbyists and the media.

In the old days of journalism, one spoke of giving a *slant* to a news article. The slant represented the writer's clearly stated or implied point-of-view and gave meaning, interest, and authenticity to the news story. Today the slant has become a spin. The intent of the spin is to cover up or mislead. It is a sanitized word for lying.

When I was a student learning the ins-and-outs of statistical methodology, it was an accepted joke about how one could lie with statistics. It was very easy to fudge the way results were presented. A current example, is George W. Bush's campaign to get an across the board reduction in taxes. He speaks of the American people receiving an average of $4,200 cut in their taxes. The fact is that a very small minority of Americans would receive such a benefit as high as that stated. A statistical

---

[15] Snyder, George E. Don't Be A Spin Sucker (Lincoln, Nebraska: Writers Club Press, 2000). P. 1.

average is a fictional number. The huge dollar reduction in the top two percent of the country's wealthy inflates the statistical average. There are two other statistical *measures of central tendency* that would give a clearer picture. One is the *mean* which is the middle point of the distribution, fifty percent above and fifty percent below. Another is the *mode* that represents the most common figure. I don't have these figures but in all likelihood the mean would be less than $450 per family. The spin doctors know this very well and they can make any story come out just the way they want it. They are practiced in employing verbal tricks. It probably would not be difficult for any one of them to write a manual on how to lie and get away with it.

It is incumbent upon us not to let them get away with it. We would be derelict in our responsibility not to be alert to others' devious efforts to gain control of our thinking. It is like the old Biblical warning to beware of false prophets. It would be stupid of us to allow our gullibility to rule our judgment.

Right-Wing Populism

As I wrote the above, I sensed a now familiar refrain. It seemed as though I was expressing a conspiracist sentiment such as is associated with survivalist, right-wing, Patriot extremists. What occurs in the broad political spectrum of our lives is a continual struggle for power. As a democratic ideal, the power lies with the people. This ideal is defined and rests in the rule of law. The Declaration of Independence, the U.S. Constitution, the Bill of Rights, and the body of legislative and judicial decisions over the years establishes what the law is and how it should be applied. How the people rule, how they express their will in accordance with the law, is a complicated matter though simplistically it occurs through the universal right to vote. The basic premise of our public life is the primacy of each individual's rights. These cannot be violated in favor of groups or the state itself.

Our system provides that there be elected representatives who maintain governance over the country's affairs. Those holding public office are sworn to uphold the law and to act in the best interests of all it's citizens. Since it is a fundamental reality of life that people do not always agree on every issue, there will be divided interests. It is natural that people will seek out those who share their points of view in an effort to fulfill their particular desires. The process results in the formation of groups for the sake of gaining power. Our laws provide for this. The exercise of power must remain within the law for a democracy to work. All too often, however, people go outside the law to achieve their own selfish interests. Doing this in league with others is to engage in a conspiracy.

When I write of politicians who knowingly distort the truth or of special interest groups who attempt to dictate how others think, I do not have in mind a grand, systematic, organized establishment. I write of strategies used by a broad range of political pressure groups. Among them are those polar forces we refer to as liberal or conservative; Democrat or Republican; left or right; radical or moderate; authoritarian or permissive; and militant or passivist. No matter what particular political persuasion one has; dishonesty, illegal acts, the abridgment of individual rights, and violation of the public trust cannot be tolerated.

There are political, ideological, and social forces at work today that are potentially destructive of the basic principles of law that define this nation. There is no single, structured group in the country that can lay claim to being the dominant threat. There are many factions that have common features, so common, in fact, that they readily form alliances. Because illegal violent acts are frequently advocated, these groups are especially dangerous. People who participate in them are not typically insane or lacking in intelligence. They do espouse ideologies and encourage behaviors that are stupid. To aid our understanding, it is helpful that at least some of these groups be identified and described.

There are several characteristics that most of the groups possess. One is Apocalyptic thinking. An associated word is millennialism. The significance of these characteristics is drawn primarily from a literalist interpretation of the New Testament's Book of Revelation. The generally understood theme goes as follows: the righteous of the world go through a time of tribulation. A powerful agent of the Devil known as the Antichrist comes to earth in league with the False Prophet. They attempt to force Christians to accept the Mark of the Beast thus denying Christ. In the End of Times there is a second coming of Christ who reclaims the righteous and restores them to a thousand years of heavenly rule. This theme is concretized in the perceived reality of the present.

How? The righteous who are to be restored to power are today's supposed innocent victims of economic and political oppression. Among them are people who believe they are being disenfranchised as citizens and being oppressed in some way or another. They are made up of the owners of small to moderate size farms, small business owners, factory workers, various kinds of laborers, the underemployed or unemployed, religious fundamentalists, and even some intelligent, well educated psychopaths.

With respect to the rural areas of our nation, particularly the farm belt, people have not shared the wealth of our recent economic boom. In the 1980's there were one million farm failures in this country. By 1990 farmers were over 200 billion dollars in debt. When farms failed in such large numbers, small town economies hit rock bottom. Nearly every business was affected from gas stations, grocery stores, to local banks. In a three year period, Iowa alone lost 5,000 retail businesses. The farm failures were no fault of the farmers. The world economy and government policy did them in. Coppola[16] writes that "by some estimates, 90 million acres—20 percent of the nation's tilled land—was lost to family farmers. As the

---

[16] Coppola, Vincent. Dragon's of God: A Journey Through Far-Right America (Marietta, Georgia: Longstreet Press, Inc., 1996). P. 67.

farms failed, new owners—the government, agribusiness, foreign conglomerates, the banks—took control." Many of these family farms, though defined as "small," consisted of as many as 3000 acres. These losses were psychologically devastating. Families were left bitter and depressed, good fodder for right-wing ideology.

Many people are frightened by current or impending societal changes. There is the concern about the undermining of family values, multi-culturalism, interracial marriages (miscegenation or "mongrelization" as some see it), and lessening of public morality. Signs of the times appeared with punk rock, rap, and such performers as Grammy Award winner Eminem whose lyrics are blatantly against blacks, women, and homosexuals. The torn, ragged, disheveled trendy dress among youth is clearly anti-establishment. It likely epitomizes doomsday attire.

There is fear of reduction in the standard of living and the loss of jobs as more opportunities are extended to third world countries. Affirmative action and increased immigration is threatening. There is a significant "brain drain" from foreign countries to the U.S. resulting in foreigners holding as many high tech jobs in this country as do Americans. There are international tensions, particularly in the middle east, and the constant threat of terrorism. The idea of a new millennium in itself raises primitive superstitious fears for many people.

Most telling is the continuing fear of major disasters such as nuclear war or terrorism by nuclear, chemical, or biological weapons. The list of potential catastrophic events seems to grow by the day. We read of environmental degradation, global warming, epidemics, and possible collision with a gigantic comet or asteroid. Movies effectively vivify images of such events.

Our country has a history of extremist political movements having a populist source that goes back to the Revolutionary War. A thorough review of that history is contained in a book by Berlet and Lyons.[17] A recent example

---

[17] Berlet, Chip and Lyons Matthew N. Right Wing Populism in America: Too Close for Comfort (New York: the Guilford Press, 2000).

showing the affects of history on rightist populism is offered by Jonathan Raban.[18] He describes the settlement of eastern Montana that began in the early 1900's by economically distressed easterners and recent immigrants from overseas. These people were duped into homesteading lands that were too barren for farming. The culprits were the owners of the newly constructed Milwaukee Railroad, the Eastern Establishment, and the U.S. Government. The motivation to attract settlers to this region served several functions. One was to help pay for the railroad. Another was to relieve the population pressures in eastern states of the unemployed in general and of new immigrants in particular. The majority of homesteads quickly failed, most before WWI, the remainder during the Great Depression. Families were worse off than they had ever been before arriving in Montana. Their only choice was to migrate further west. They went to western Montana, Idaho, Washington, and California. They were bitter people, distrusting of big business and the federal government. They prized having independence and living off the land if it were at all possible. They became rugged individualists as did their offspring. The eastern slopes of the Rocky Mountains and other parts of western Montana offered the opportunity for them to engage in this relatively unique lifestyle. It is no accident that in recent times the area became the home of the Montana Freeman, the Church Universal and Triumphant, and Ted Kaczynski.

What of the modern day oppressors? They are regarded as the Antichrist. Included are what has been called the Eastern Establishment. These are the super-wealthy who control the economy and have undue influence upon government. Many who claim being oppressed believe Jews are instrumental in conducting a campaign of world domination. Instruments of the federal government such as the IRS, FBI, the ATF (Alcohol, Tobacco, and Firearms bureau), and FEMA (Federal Emergency Management Administration) are regarded as enemies. Also included are

---

18 Raban, Jonathan. Bad Land: An American Romance (London, England: Picador, 1997).

the liberal media and the WTO (World Trade Organization) and the UN itself. The U.S. Government is viewed by many as the *New Evil Empire.*

There has been a certain degree of blending between the religious and secular right. Some of the secular survivalist groups have adopted the Apocalyptic myth and religious groups have assumed a survivalist and paramilitary mentality. Morris Dees[19] reports that between the mid 1990's there were 441 survivalist/militia type groups in the U.S. There were at least one in every state. Additionally, there were 368 groups actively engaged in providing ideological support. They called themselves Patriots. A good number of the "groups" are one person who publishes a newsletter and has a web site. Others, however, have memberships that number in the thousands. A recent estimate is that approximately five million individuals have united in their belief that the government is secretly planning to impose tyrannical control over the country. Modern electronic technology enables various groups not only to propagandize and recruit new members but it allows them to coordinate their activities, whether ideological, political, or criminal.

Among the identifiable groups are the traditional ones such as the KKK, the John Birch Society, and the American Nazi Party. Ones that have gotten a good deal of publicity are the Branch Dividians led by David Koresh, the Church Universal and Triumphant of "Guru Ma," and the Montana Freeman whose chief spokesman is John Trochmann. The Branch Dividian compound in Waco, Texas was destroyed by a Federal task force on April 19, 1993. Along with Koresh, 73 adults and 21 children died, probably resigned to the fact that they had reached the End of Times. Four Federal agents also were murdered.

"Guru Ma" expressed her apocalyptic viewpoint as follows: "God destroys the ruling powers of evil and raises the righteous to life in a

---

[19] Dees, Morris with Corcoran, James. *Gathering Storm: America's Militia Threat* (New York: HarperCollings Publisher, 1996). P. 201.

messianic kingdom that will last 1,000 years—the prophesied millennium."[20] Her following resides on a 30,000 acre property on the northern border of Yellowstone National Park. "In the Fall of 1989, Edward Francis, husband of Elizabeth Clare Prophet and vice president of the church, was convicted of illegally purchasing $100,000 worth of semiautomatic weapons and handguns and 120,000 rounds of ammunition under a false name."[21]

The Montana Freeman had a run in with local law enforcement in 1996. This group believed in "common law," declaring that the U.S. Constitution was invalid because of its Jewish influence. They declared themselves free from paying income taxes, registering their automobiles with the state, and honoring court orders to vacate foreclosed and auctioned off property. Berlet and Lyons[22] cite John Trochmann talking at a recent lecture tour about Jews being in league with Satan and that Blacks and other persons of color as subhuman.

One very vocal group is that known as the Christian Identity movement. It is a quasi-religious organization founded in 1946 by Wesley Smith. It articulates the underlying philosophy of numerous extremist groups. Their claim is that the United States is the real promised land and that "White Christians are the real children of Israel."[23] The same authors go on to quote Leonard Zeskind that "...Jews are children of Satan, while African Americans and other people of color are subhuman: they are 'pre-Adamic' mud people—'God's failures before perfecting Adam.'" How God's imperfection can be reconciled with Christianity remains a mystery.

---

[20] Lamy, Philip. Millennium Rage: Survivalists, White Supremacists, and the Doomsday Prophecy (New York: Plenum Press, 1996). P. 3.

[21] *Ibid.* P. 2.

[22] *Op Cite.* P. 295.

[23] *Op Cite.* Berlet and Lyons. P. 270.

In his book *Close Encounters with the Religious Right*, Boston[24] describes his several years of first hand experience with extreme fundamentalists. He mentions his feelings when attending their various meetings. To him it was an immediate reaction of being in a *twilight zone*. The sensation is one of "I can't believe my ears" when hearing the diatribe. He points out how many of the followers are "good" people—not the typical hatemonger. Boston remarks how he is always amazed at people's gullibility, low level of skepticism, swallowers of everything, and absolutists in their thinking. He concludes that "good" people all too readily follow "bad" leaders and "bad" ideologies.

In Boston's own words, he wanted "to get up close and personal" with religious rightist groups. He became practically an insider over a twelve year period of attending meetings, viewing TV evangelists, and studying their literature. Among those he focused on were Pat Robertson, Jerry Falwall, James Dobson and their associates. His revelations show just how dangerous right-wing, politico-religious groups can be. Here is a sampling of some of their objectives beyond the simple refrain of most right-wingers, a refrain that goes against pro-choice, homosexuals, Jews, non-whites, secular humanists, and the liberal establishment.

The most insidious strategy is to destroy the barrier between church and state. Boston heard a religious right speaker say with regard to church-state separation that it was "the sharpest sword in the devil's arsenal (p. 48)." By far the greatest amount of effort on the part of the various groups investigated was to get fundamentalists elected to political offices. Such offices included public school boards and the various levels of elected positions from local leaders to the presidency. Recently, the religious right claimed having control over Republican leadership in half the states and strong inroads into the others.

---

[24] Boston, Robert. Close Encounters with the Religious Right: Journeys into the Twilight Zone of Religion and Politics (New York: Prometheus Books, 2000).

Close on the heals of this threat is the opposition to public schools. Boston quotes the following from religious right literature: "[public schools are] satanic imitations of the true God's institutional church (p.143)." A plea from far-right activists called upon all evangelical Christians to withdraw their children from public schools (p. 58). Little wonder that part of their political agenda is to get public funding of school vouchers. Related to this assault on our public schools is the insistence upon school sponsored prayer and the posting of the Ten Commandments in schools and other public buildings.

As mentioned previously, Boston found his attendance at religious right gatherings to be chilling. The prime reason for his reacting so was the prevalence of meanness among speakers and attendees. At times he feared for his own safety. He could not reconcile such utterances as the following with the teachings of Jesus Christ. Here is a sampling of what Boston calls Religious Right Rage. "We must use our spiritual bayonets. We must use bayonets, for the nation must be taken for the love of God (P. 51)." "We must resolve to conquer or die (p. 61)." A speaker at the 1999 "Road to Victory" meeting shouted "We are at war! We are at war! (p. 91)."

Most damning of all is the religious right's embracing of Christian Reconstructionism. This is "the far-right philosophy that holds that the United States's laws should be based on the harsh legal code of the Old Testament, which ought to be read literally (i.e. blasphemers, adulterers, 'incorrigible' teenagers, and the 'unchaste' get the death penalty."

Lyon[25] writes that "the millennial myth [apocalyptic belief] is so flexible in its ability to adapt to modern times that it has been invoked by many groups and even by the mass media and popular culture to explain contemporary events..."

To comprehend the modern looseness of associations to the Biblical apocryphal story, it is helpful to examine the text itself. Over a hundred

---

[25] *Op Cite*. Lyons. P. 262.

years of Biblical scholarship puts the interpretation of the Book of Revelation in its proper context. It was authored by John of Patmos in the year 95 C.E. (the common era), not the John who wrote the fourth and last Gospel. He lived and suffered under the rule of the Roman emperor Domitian. John was steeped in Old Testament and Apocryphal writings. These were rich in the Apocalyptic story going back as early as 200 B.C.E. (before the common era). The Jewish people were firm in their belief that they were God's chosen people. They felt it was their destiny to eventually rule the world as God would have it. However, their repeated experience as a nation was of total oppression and destruction. The world order as they came to view it was utterly evil and beyond being reformed. They conceived of the world's history as being divided into two ages: the horrible present and the age to come. God would see to it that the present world would be destroyed and replaced by one as glorious as the Garden of Eden.

In 95 C.E. when the Book of Revelation was composed, Christians were undergoing extreme persecution at the hands of Roman authorities. Earlier under Nero and later under Domitian, torture and execution of Jews and Christians was both a political act and a sport. Since they could not bring themselves to swear annually that Caesar was Lord they were summarily executed, often in the cruelest of ways. Though the affirmation that Caesar was Lord was meant to insure political allegiance to Rome, Jews and Christians could not divorce the act from its religious meaning.

The message of the Book of Revelations was seditious under Roman rule. Consequently, the ideas expressed were coded. The intended readers of that day had a key to the code, a key we no longer have. The code takes the form of myth and metaphor. The writer was a Christian having some hostility towards Jews but he was himself reared as a Jew and was steeped in Jewish sacred literature and liturgy. As was common for New Testament writing, the Book of Revelations drew heavily on the Jewish tradition. John of Patmos, scholar of the Old Testament, borrowed metaphor after metaphor in composing Revelations. Because of the heavy use of metaphor we find this book to be the most puzzling of all contained in the Bible. As beautifully expressed as poetry, the book was subject to whatever meaning later readers wished it to contain. In its historical context it was a message of hope to Christians that they were to endure persecution until their enemies were destroyed by acts of God. They would be spared and elevated along with the deserving dead to a heavenly existence much like the Garden of Eden.

A second shared characteristic of these right-wing, extremist groups is related to the old Protestant Work Ethic. The work ethic dictates that one earn his own keep. One must travail to further himself and to provide for his family and community. Engaging in constructive activities is owed. Elizabeth Barrett Browning wrote that "free men freely work: whoever fears God, fears to sit at ease." Work and toil was regarded since the time of the Pilgrims as a godly activity. It is no accident that sloth is one of the seven deadly sins.

Our third president, Thomas Jefferson, thought that the highest vocation was that of farming. He believed that the farmer was the backbone of our democratic society. His belief was that they exemplified the ultimate nobleness of moral character as well as having contributed to our economic base. For many, the expression "good, honest work" meant manual labor that resulted in a tangible product.

Berlet and Lyons write that a fundamental belief of "right-wing populist ideology has been *producerism,* a doctrine that champions the so-called producers in society against both 'unproductive' elites and subordinate groups defined as lazy or immoral." Among the producers are farmers, laborers, artisans or craftsmen, those engaged in manufacturing, and construction workers. It is interesting to note the sporting preference of hunting and fishing over that of golf. Hunting in particular is the expression of the fantasy of being independent and providing for one's

---

[26] *Op Cite.* P. 6.

own nourishment. It meets the dream of many a macho man "of living off the land." Golf on the other hand was a "gentleman's sport." It was for the country club crowd. (This is a blurred image, of course, because we have for years had public links, and celebrity professional golfers commonly emerged from the ranks of caddies or children of club pros).

Among the non-producers are the elitist power brokers of New York City. Bankers, speculators, and monopolists fall into this class. Also included would be "intellectuals," writers, educators, movie stars (except John Wayne and Charlton Heston), and TV news anchors. Bureaucrats and other public servants appointed or elected are non-producers. At the bottom of the list are street people, people on welfare, the shiftless unemployed, Blacks, and low-life foreigners. All these are regarded as not contributing to the public good in any material way. They are seen as living off the sweat of the working man.

Producerism helps to distinguish the amorphous "we the people" from *they*, the elitist who are oppressors. The elitist are those who at any given time are in control of our nation. The most enduring of the elitist are those *behind the scenes* who pull the strings of politicians, administrators, and others who control the economy.

The *behind the scenes* notion leads to a third distinguishing characteristic of the right-wing extremist. It is the mode of thinking best described as *conspiracism*. It thrives on suspiciousness, distrust, and paranoid ideation. Systematic scenarios are construed in which others are secretly plotting to take advantage of, control, or destroy "us." It involves scapegoating in that there is a target group. (Scapegoating stems from the laying of one's sins on the sacrificial goat thus absolving oneself from condemnation). A conspiracy can be scripted by the elite as well as from the non-elite. One example of the former occurred when the last Russian Czar labeled the Jews as a threat to the monarchy and had them killed or run off (evidenced in the theme of "Fiddler on the Roof"). Another example, of course, occurred when Hitler raged against the Jews as being deserving of extermination. Jews along with Catholics, the Irish, Blacks, Native Americans, Asians, Hispanics, and other minority groups have at various times been scapegoated in this country. Current right-wing groups defined as non-elite are particularly prone to target Jews, Blacks, and homosexuals.

This right-wing scapegoating is particularly venomous. The "enemy" is viewed as having all-embracing power that controls every meaningful detail of our lives. They are seen as hell-bent on determining that our nation be controlled by a Jewish led New World Order. Another aspect of the right-winger is described by Berlet and Lyons[27] as follows: "[they] frame social conflict in terms of a transcendent struggle between Good and Evil that reflects the influence of the apocalyptic paradigm." A third trait is to see the conspiracy as a "vast" plot and the supporting evidence is greatly exaggerated or fabricated. An illustration is to maintain that the supermarket bar codes is a way the Antichrist is able to give people The Mark of the Beast, the dreaded number 666. Another is to believe that the government is carrying out a plan to implant microchips in all new born infants so that in the future the authorities will always know where people are.

A fourth measure characteristically used by the rightist is a progression of twisted thinking leading from marginalization to demonization and scapegoating. As the name suggests, marginalizing is establishing a boundary between groups, separating them on the basis of belonging or not belonging. Not belonging is to be an "outsider" and to be undesirable. It leads to the separation of "us" versus "them." The remark about "those people" sometimes made by errant politicians such as Ross Perot raises the hackles of the referenced people.

To be an outsider is not to possess the "good," desirable qualities that are supposed to distinguish the in-group. On the contrary, outsider members have distasteful and objectionable traits of looking different, dressing differently, behaving differently, talking differently, listening to different music, eating different foods, etc. Worse, they worship differently and

---

[27] *Op Cite.* P. 10.

hold dangerous ideas and values. Taking special note of foreign character-istics is sometimes an exaggeration through over-generalization and some-times they are outright fabrications. We hear say: "Italians smell of garlic," "Irishmen are lushes," and "Blacks are mentally inferior."

The next step in this thought progression is likely to be dehumaniza-tion. "They" are said not to be human. Rather, those we have distanced ourselves from are a sub-human species. At the simplest level, this process is the "I-Thou" versus the "I-It" described so well by Martin Buber.[28] Those we accept as family, friends, and colleagues are related to as persons: such a one is a Thou. Others are viewed as objects or things: such a one is an It. An ordinary encounter with the cashier at the neighborhood 7-Eleven can be a person-to-person interaction or it can be an "I" engaged with an automaton performing a ritualized function.

At a more devastating level we note the not-so-long-ago expression that the "only good Indian is a dead Indian." The Black slavery tradition, own-ing human beings as property, made the dehumanizing process easier for many people. During the Holocaust, the bodies of exterminated Jews were laid out in long piles like cord wood.

Dehumanizing others made it so much easier to persecute and to mur-der them. Belief in demonization helped to assuage a conscience if one existed. This process ascribes evilness to one's targeted victims. A class of people are regarded as agents of Satan. They are said to be the Antichrist bent on destroying the cherished world of the persecutors. Allusions are frequently made to vipers and the dragons of the Book of Revelations.

Perhaps the greatest danger from the right-wing extremists is the subtle effect it has on the wider public. Religious beliefs such as those advocated by Jerry Falwell and Pat Robertson are made to look less threatening by comparison. Political parties are moving toward "the center" in order to get sufficient votes to obtain offices. The source of this movement is the

---

[28] Kaufmann, Walter. I and Thou: Martin Buber: A New Translation (New York: Charles Scribner's Sons, 1970).

extreme pressure from the right. The pressure impinges on both our major political parties. Some have said that Al Gore lost the presidency because he was too far left of center. When he advocated further measures of gun control, expressed anti-smoking sentiment, and favored women's right to choose, he was being too liberal for many people's taste. It is for these reasons that he lost the vote in Arkansas, West Virginia and his own state of Tennessee. If he had won any one of these states, he would have become the president in 2000. Some have suggested that Republicans have embraced the disparate far right groups both religious and secular in order to gain a majority at the polls. This effort might be sanitized by the label of being "inclusive."

A few years back a well known fast food chain had a TV commercial showing three elderly ladies standing at the service counter holding out a hamburger and questioning in an irritating, demanding tone "where's the beef?" We might ask the same question of the right-winger. Where's the beef or what's the beef? We know that they carry within them deep fears and anxieties. They feel impotent by not having the means to control their own destiny. But what is it that is such a great threat to them? To this point I have cited a number of examples such as restriction on gun ownership and use of Federal funds for birth control clinics. These sources of discontent are arguable. Unfortunately, some of what fuels their fire are complex systemic ills. These fall within the areas of social, economic, and political realms both at a national and international level. They are issues that resonate within a vast number of thoughtful people, perhaps even a majority of Americans. Among such issues are a more equitable distribution of wealth; reformed political campaign financing; and universal health care. Progress in solving such problems has been slow to non-existent. Many are frustrated. Fortunately, most dedicate themselves to bringing about reform through legitimate avenues. Some of the wailing from the extreme right-wing, however, gains widespread sympathy when they are listened to.

When smart people do stupid things, we usually assume that it's the result of faulty decision making. The following chapter explores this idea further by looking at the question of free will.

Chapter *III*

Do We Really Choose?

Age Old Question of Freewill Versus Determinism

Here we have a question that has been debated for centuries. We will explore the roots of the argument of freewill versus determinism. We also will look at an important related question. That question has to do with the broad behavioral phenomena of self-control. If there is free will then we should be able to exercise self-control. We generally believe from personal experience that people vary considerably within themselves and from one person to another as to how well they are able to manage their own behavior. It is important that this also be examined.

Free will is a concept that most of us find we understand without further explanation. Our gut level response is "yes, of course, I am able to make choices." However, our legal system for one does not find it to be obvious in all instances. We also at times find ourselves puzzling over people who are substance abusers. They seem obviously out of control in managing their lives. Are they to be held morally, legally, and medically responsible (that is responsible for their own treatment)? Is the juvenile delinquent to be excused because he was reared in a dysfunctional family?

50

Discussing whether such a thing as free will exists is more than an intellectual exercise as the above examples indicate. Pursuance of this concept involves philosophical, scientific, and psychological arguments.

Let us first look at the concept of determinism. According to Weatherford[29] determinism means "that all our mental states and acts, including choices and decisions, and all our actions are effects necessitated by preceding causes." That is to say that future events are as fixed and unchangeable as the past is fixed and unchangeable. What happens in this world is all that could happen, there being no potential realizable alternatives.

Mechanical determinism emerges from the principle that everything has a cause. The simple proposition is if *a*, then *b*. When *a* occurs, whatever it may be, it is *sufficient* to cause the event of *b*. When *b* occurs it is the *necessary* consequence of *a*. When I flip on the light switch, the light bulb illuminates the room. The flipping of the switch is a sufficient cause for the bulb to be activated. For the bulb to turn on, it is necessary that the switch be flipped.

It is presumed that one cause leads to another as with the connected links of a chain having interminable length. Causality thus appears as an infinite regression. The movement of the light switch makes a connection between a flexible copper strip and a copper wire terminal. Now the *a* is the copper strip and the *b* is the wire terminal. The touching of the two copper components allows for the flow of an electrical current, one commonly regarded as positively charged. The *a* is the contact of the two terminals and the *b* is the flow of current, and so on.

One cause may have multiple effects. I could have had the light switch activate simultaneously both the light and the stereo player. The most common characteristics of events is that they have multiple causes. One

---

[29] Weatherford, Roy C. "Freedom and Determinism" in The Oxford Companion to Philosophy [Ed. By Honderich, Ted] (New York: Oxford University Press, 1995). P. 292.

might then say that a paired relationship is a component of a number of other pairs that jointly and of necessity leads to a particular effect. This can become quite complicated by what is known as interactive effects. When two or more pairs are contingent a reciprocal effect may occur. The interaction may become an element of the effective cause.

In the light switch example, I didn't mention the fact that it was I who turned the switch. What determined my flipping the switch? It might be said that the room was dark and thus I was compelled to turn the light on. As a creature with limited night vision, it would be problematic for me to try to negotiate my way around the room in the dark. A complex causative and deterministic chain could be made of this. When we get away from mechanical causality into the human condition we heap one complexity upon another. We might scoff at the miscreant who claims that "the Devil made me do it." However, we might have to ponder over the assertion that "my parents set a bad example for me."

The Greek philosopher, Aristotle (384-322 B.C.E.), launched the argument concerning free-will when he wished to explain the problem of evil. If God were omnipotent and God were good why should there be evil? His answer was that men possessed a degree of free-will. Thus man was responsible for the evil in the world.

By freedom is meant the ability to initiate a new beginning, being able to break with the past. It amounts to self-determination. It permits creativity. It allows for responsibility. One can take credit and be given credit for acts that are either generous or onerous.

The past is present and as such it provides continuity, direction, and control to a degree. Consciousness of the past enables us to have self-awareness, to sense a presence of mind. This function we label as mind allows us to move outside of the past into the here and now and imagine the future. The mind can weigh the influence of the past and the relevance of the present and future and allow itself to be swayed one way or another.

Some recent thinking on the subject[30] of free-will removes the concept from that of determinism. The source of free-will may be determined, be a matter of chance, or be from some third, unknown cause.

The issue of free-will is critical in distinguishing a fully human person from a non-functioning individual or from sub-human species. We have heard that the presence of rationality separates man from other living things. Although being rational is a prerequisite, it is not a sufficient distinguishing feature for defining a human. Free-will must co-exist. We also have been told that self-awareness sets man apart from animals. We may ask what is there about self-awareness that is so significant? The answer is that free-will is the vital component.

Free-will must be differentiated from freedom of action. Exercising free-will is not having the freedom to do whatever you want. There may be constraints on our actions such as being physically confined or inhibited by some sort of social pressure.

Free-will is "[freedom] to will what you want to will...."[31] (One can do so even while imprisoned). The man who exercises free-will can reflect upon and evaluate his wants and don't wants. If because of constraint effective action is not implemented, free-will permits their being a possibility and potential that may or may not subsequently be realized.

Those incapable of free-will are nevertheless motivated to act from want. A chimpanzee is wanting to obtain a meal of ants. He employs his elementary reasoning powers to locate an ant hill. He even secures a tool in the form of a stick. With the stick, he agitates the ants in the mound of earth and conveys them to his mouth. The chimp experiences a want and acts upon it. He wants to eat something palatable and does so given freedom of action. The chimpanzee does not have free-will. He can't reflect upon and evaluate his wants. He can't think about doing one thing and

---

[30] Frankfurt, Harry G. "Freedom of the Will and the Concept of a Person." In Rosenthal, David M. The Nature of Mind (New York: Oxford University Press, 1991).

[31] *Ibid.* P. 445.

also entertain the possibility of doing something else. He can't decide to eat ants one day and grubs the next.

Man on the other hand has an awareness of his wants and he can freely structure them. He can decide what he wants or doesn't want. He can organize his wanting food. He can choose to have three square meals a day. He can decide on what to eat and where.

The concept of free-will is tied to our ideas about responsibility. A man who is a habitual smoker craves a cigarette. He wants to smoke one. On the other hand, he knows that smoking is harmful to his health so he wants not to smoke. His habituation brings about effective action—he smokes in spite of not wanting to. The fact that he wants not to smoke and yet does leads him to say that there is a force beyond himself that determines his behavior. The force he feels is against his will. Thus in this matter, he lacks free-will. If this could be construed as a moral issue, he would not be held responsible.

Contrariwise, a willing smoker, one who wills to smoke without reservation, may be labeled morally responsible. It is presumed that he had free-will to will otherwise—not to be desirous of maintaining the smoking habit.

Free will enables us to choose regardless of compulsion, external influences and pressures, rationality, or deep personal conviction. The exercising of free will can be thought of as volunteerism. For any given act one is able to say "I would have done otherwise if I had so chosen."[32]

We cannot find an entity or location for the function we call "will." Possibly in time microbiologists and neurologists will find areas in the brain that appear to mediate willfulness. If they do, they will have further evidence to link psychic phenomena to our physical being and thus introduce a new argument for determinism. We describe our faculty for free-will as governing acts of volition such as choosing, deciding, releasing, and

---

[32] *Op Cite*. Weatherford. P. 292.

energizing our musculature. It lies at the center of what makes us an individual and, thus, it determines personhood.

What about the connection of free-will with self control? A strong argument for the presence of free-will lies in Darwinism. Evolution is a function of three variables: reproduction, variation, and selection. It occurs at a sub-atomic level as well as at the molecular level. Variation appears to be largely chance based on genetic mutations. Thus chance plays a part in the microscopic world as well as in the macro world of complex living beings. Evolution is attributable to natural, deterministic laws and chance. Selection is a critical part of the evolutionary process and it rests upon the rule of survival of the fittest. The environment in which we live is constantly changing. Sometimes change is gradual, measured in hundreds of thousands of years. At other times there can be cataclysmic events that bring about change in a thousand years or less. It seems that life has moved from the relatively simple to increasing complexity. The increase in complexity has allowed for greater variability and flexibility. The human mind is at the pinnacle of the evolutionary ladder and free-will hones our capacity for coping with change. There is a consensus that what distinguishes us from animals is the ability to make conscious decisions, freeing us from the bonds of instinct.

When thinking about human activity at the behavioral level we can see how habits of mind and muscle direct many of our actions. Impulses and compulsions seem to emerge from some primitive instinctual well of drives that have the characteristics of determinism. But as long as the sensorium and central nervous system are intact and functioning normally, we can expect that reason is in command and that free-will may be exercised when judgments are in order. Thus it is that we think of having self-control.

Aristotle defined self-control as the ability to conduct oneself according to his best judgment when confronted with contrary temptations. It is the capacity to resist any motivational state that is in conflict with one's values, principles, or judgments. The judgments may rest upon the practical as well as the hypothetical. They may stem from the theoretical or empirical. Judgment is the ability to resist the deterministic quality of unconscious urges and whims.

We tend to think of self-control only in a positive sense (the same being true of free-will). In reality, as a concept, it is of neutral value. One in possession of self-control can be a saint or a rogue. It is a matter of the guiding values one adheres to. We would dread a contest with a cool, calculating, disciplined, amoral opponent.

When we search for the origins within the human psyche of an executive-type control, we could look at Sigmund Freud's conceptualization of the *Ego*. He viewed it as the part of the psychic apparatus that mediated between the person and reality. It enabled one to perceive reality and make accommodating adjustments. It originates in the human organism, gradually determined partly by maturation and partly by learning.

Following birth and in the earliest stages of infancy, the baby has awareness but doesn't differentiate its ego from anything in the external world. Every experience is assessed in terms of the pleasure or displeasure of having its needs fulfilled upon demand. Feeding whether by being held and fed a bottle or being nursed at the mother's breast is associated with its own body functions. Ego development only begins when instinctual needs (at this time sensed as survival needs) are frustrated. According to psychoanalytic theory, when some of the objects in the environment do not respond as desired, there is a dawning consciousness of an external world and the preexisting sense of omnipotence begins to dissolve. The early frustrations are the basis of what psychoanalysts call primary anxiety. It is what later philosophers regard as existential anxiety, a lifelong component of our being. In time the infant becomes more active in coping with external objects. As the parents provide for its needs, they are taken in to become part of the baby's own being. Thus in this way, the infant attempts to maintain a sense of omnipotence. This period of development leaves a remnant within the matured personality of primitive, magical thinking. In time reality presses itself upon the subjective experience of the infant to the extent that the ego has to assume ever increasing control. Active mastery "is achieved through the interposing of time, the development of a tension tolerance, and the development of judgment (the ability to anticipate the future in the imagination by testing reality)."[33] There is a leap forward in impulse control with the development of language. Speech greatly facilitates thinking. Thinking as an anticipatory act makes reality testing possible without great risk. The imaging that went on before the development of language was regarded as "primary process" thinking. That which followed was called "secondary process." Thus, we find that "…prelogical thinking will be used as a substitute for logical thinking only when the latter cannot master unpleasant reality."[34] Examples of primary process thinking would include magical thinking and superstition.

Coping with reality is facilitated by the developing ego's ability to delay or totally inhibit immediate gratification of impulses. This sets the *pleasure principle* against the *reality principle*. The ability to delay gratification, the reality principle, is the major index of maturity and socialization.

The Freudian conceptualization as described is a metaphor. Its scientific underpinnings come primarily from anecdotal reporting and interpretation. However, it is useful as metaphors are in rendering a clearer picture of what we know to be a very complicated process.

Psychologists espousing behaviorist theory would formulate a different explanation. Theirs would consist of conditioning through stimulus-response connections. These can be ever more complicated as the theory unfolds. However, to put it simply, the process is that of learning and conditioning. The idea of a mediating entity such as an ego or self can be discarded as far as a strict behaviorist is concerned.

Carl Jung makes a meaningful distinction between ego and self. The ego concept in the Freudian sense is very circumscribed. It relates simply

---

33 Hinsie, Leland E. and Campbell, Robert J. Psychiatric Dictionary (New York: Oxford University Press, 1970). P. 248.

34 *Ibid.*

to the mediator between the individual and reality. Jung views the ego as a complexity of stored images and it along with many other associated mental processes (particularly the unconscious), together at a global level, defines the self.

Self-control appears to depend on that element of mental functioning we described as the executive function and the broader element we commonly regard as the self-concept. We must follow Jung's lead and incorporate into the idea of self the global aspects of self-esteem, self-confidence, conscience, acquired tastes, and values to mention a few. The acquisition of skills and knowledge are what appear to be crucial in the matter of self-control. To put it in a nut shell, we can speak of learning.

Some forms of learning probably begin in the later stages of fetal development. They obviously continue during early infancy. As language begins (and this may be earlier than we ever dreamed because of recent evidence of infants responding to sign language), the possibilities for learning take a quantum leap. The young are very imitative organisms. They will learn by mimicking, modeling themselves from the behaviors of those around them. Thus, we hear of the importance of role models in children's lives. It certainly begins with parents.

Children learn from their siblings, from other children, and from adults other than their parents. They usually learn at a very early age from what they see on TV. This experience typically precedes by a few years the child's first exposure to formal schooling. Most of their TV learning is haphazard because much of it is unsupervised. Children have to supply their own meaning and understanding to their viewing since the messages aren't guided and placed in appropriate context by a wise adult. The same is true to the extent that a child is involved in the use of computer games and the Internet.

Acquiring self-control through learning rests upon modeling and appropriate teaching. It is unfortunate that there is great disparity among children as to whether they receive appropriate and constructive teaching. If they are reared in poverty, in a single parent family, in a bi-lingual environment, and in a minority group that suffers from discrimination of various sorts they are going to have a tougher time in getting a good start in life. If their schools are sub-par for whatever reason they will suffer accordingly.

There are some basic things that children must be taught to obtain self-control. First of all they must have the opportunity to gain a sense of mastery over some significant aspect of their lives. They have to be good at something and get recognition and appreciation for it. The positives that come from demonstrated mastery must not be overshadowed by negative reinforcements. These come by way of unmet expectations followed by derogatory and humiliating responses from others. We see the joys of mastery from very early in life when children develop the skills of self-feeding, crawling, standing, walking, and climbing. When still very young, they learn to dress themselves, wash their hands and faces, brush their teeth, help in the selection of their own clothes, and so on. In nursery school or kindergarten, they learn to cooperate with other children their own age. They learn to discriminate various materials according to such abstractions as size, shape, and color. They learn to draw, paint, and beat rhythmically on a triangle or tambourine. They learn to throw a ball, dodge it, and kick it for some distance in a desired direction. All such things and many, many more lead to a sense of mastery. Mostly, children need only be given the opportunity to do things *on their own.* Encouragement from others is OK as is appreciation. Teachers open the doors of opportunity by framing tasks, demonstrating needed skills, and conveying information. Children respond by working out the solutions, taking pride in their accomplishments, and acquiring a sense of independence.

Besides mastery, children should learn certain things about themselves and others. They need to care about themselves and be relatively comfortable with who they are. This depends greatly on whether or not they are loved and are deemed lovable by significant adults. The love they receive has to be of a special quality. It need be what is referred to as unconditional love. "You are worthy just because you are you" is the message of unconditional love. Being prized is not dependent upon approval for specific or general acts or characteristics. The child need not feel "bad" for messing his diapers, spilling a glass of milk, getting a lesser grade than hoped for on his report card, or not being athletic.

The child must learn how to get along with others, with children of all ages and adults. Modeling goes a long way for this to occur. The significant adults in his life must treat him respectfully and understandingly. The "golden rule" can be demonstrated as well as explained. Sometimes modeling is not enough. There must be a conscious effort to instill habits of sharing, cooperating, negotiating, and conducting amicable conflict resolutions. An ethic of unselfishness must be instilled. Ethics, morals, and values play such a significant role in self-control because of the following: *A contentious individual, regardless of reasons, can no longer exercise self-control or free will. He unleashes forces of his own making external to himself that determine his future.* Simply put, by one's own actions one can relinquish his free-will.

Self-control rests upon learning how to approach problems in a rational manner. A child has to learn to think critically. He can rediscover the distinctions made by Plato over two thousand years ago—the difference between reason, passion, and appetite. Plato's moral was to achieve balance between the three elements. True understanding between persons is achieved by weighing the fact that every human communication consists of a cognitive message, feelings, and needs. The communicants must *hear* one another in the context of messages intended with their associated feelings.

Blind reliance on authority is obviously yielding one's own powers of reason and free choice. Hopefully, a child can acquire the simple moral contained in the question "does it make sense to you?" Seldom is a child appeased by such parental declarations as "because I told you so" or "do as I say" and that is how it should be.

Children need to recognize the fallacies of over-generalizations and absolutes. The "all's" and "none's" as well as the "always" and "never's" seldom ring true.

Literalism is an abomination. We should thank God for Santa Clause. It is a fable we love for our children to believe in. Jolly old St. Nick and his reindeer each year brings a reminder of love, peace, joy, and happiness. Much of this is expressed by generous giving and song. We hate to see children denied the experience of this fable. Rare is the adult who doesn't have warm, fond memories of his childhood Christmases. The second blessing of this childhood fable is that as children mature they discover that *it is a fable*. It was not factual in the sense that George Washington was our first president. Likewise, nursery school rhymes are fantasy. "Humpty Dumpty had a great fall....could not put Humpty Dumpty together again." Not so sad because Humpty Dumpty was an egg. Micky Mouse is not human. He is not even a mouse. He is what we call a cartoon character. So it should not be so difficult for children to learn about fictional characters, cartoons, fables, nursery rhymes, similes, metaphors, parables, or myths. They cannot be taken as the literal truth.

In the sense that they don't reflect reality, old wives tales and superstitions share common ground with figures of speech. They fall into the category of pre-logical thinking such as that referred to by Freud. Behavioral psychologists have demonstrated the formation of superstitious beliefs as the consequence of accidental contingencies. The basketball player at the free-throw line always tugs at his shorts with his right hand before launching the ball toward the basket. He believes that if he doesn't it won't go in. He believes it so strongly that it probably wouldn't.

The nature of rumor and propaganda can be taught. One can learn ways to recognize them and evaluate them objectively. Raise the question "where is the evidence?"

The above mentioned examples having to do with objective reasoning play an important role, if not an essential one, in the exercise of free-will and self-control. One can freely choose when constraints on clear thinking are lifted.

Nature of Choice

Choice is essentially synonymous with decision making. The word decision is derived from the Latin *decidere*. It means to cut through or cut off. When one decides one makes a break with the past and takes a step into the future. One must give something of the past up, something of the familiar and comfortable. The future leads to the unfamiliar and challenging. This oftentimes requires courage. To exercise free will then calls upon one's strength of character.

Choice Socially Constrained

When a situation demands our having to rely on our own reasoning powers, there is often a good deal of external pressure to think conventionally. "Don't break with tradition!" "Be loyal to family, group, team, or country!" "Don't be a party pooper." Such may be the pleas for us to follow rather than go on our own volition. It takes courage to think and choose for oneself in the face of social duress.

We learn that the major reason for children smoking is because of peer pressure. For a junior high school student to be bombarded with taunts and razzing from his schoolmates for refusing cigarettes or drugs, is difficult to put up with. Perhaps the most important secondary reason for a child smoking is the influence of cigarette advertizing. This too requires that the child think for him or herself. This is a real challenge for the young mind. Interestingly, one recent strategy that has met with some success against teens smoking is to demonstrate how the tobacco industry is exploiting them. No one likes to be manipulated. Not being manipulated is to retain the power of choosing for oneself.

Classes of Behavior Where Free Choice is in Doubt

There are a great number of other factors that can impede our ability to exercise free-will and to maintain self-control. Among them are a variety of psychological components such as impulsiveness, compulsions, and habituation. The very nature of impulsive behavior is that it is beyond rational control. It is initiated either by organic or psychic stimuli within the person. If the impulse emerges from an instinctual source, it lies within the unconscious. If it originates from the psyche and is conscious, some form of ideation acts as a triggering mechanism. Action follows automatically bypassing judgement.

Compulsions are repetitive behaviors having a ritualistic form. The individual acting compulsively is aware of what he is doing but is unable to consciously resist it. In fact he wishes not to engage in the act but feels powerless to resist it. Any partially successful resistance leads to mounting tension. This will reach the point when delay is no longer possible. The sudden release of this tension will be immediately gratifying and it will satisfy for a period of time. The types of acts are usually inconsequential in and of themselves. An example would be a man who can never turn a door knob without first coughing once followed by clearing his throat twice. The dynamics behind compulsions relate to unconscious conflicts. The conflict is expressed in this peculiarly disguised form.

It has often been said that people are creatures of habit. Unfortunately, there are times when they become victims of habit. Examples are biting fingernails, thumb sucking, pulling one's hair, and nose picking. These are unlike addictions such as smoking and they are not compulsions because they aren't an expression of unconscious conflicts. Clearly, however, they are undesirable for the one habituated and they seem to be beyond one's power to stop. They are formed for various reasons. Thumb sucking can be a substitute gratification for sucking at a nipple or pacifier. Nail biting might be accidentally associated with tension reduction. Unfortunately, it like some other habits, becomes its own reward. Refraining from following through on the habit builds tension. Doing it releases this tension and it is thus positively reinforced.

Commonly, a habit is associated with a particular time and place. Obviously, thumb sucking is most frequently a ritual before falling asleep at night. Nail biting can be restricted to times when talking on the telephone. One might tug at his hair while reading a book to such an extent that a bald spot will appear.

Abdication of Responsibility

We can abdicate our responsibility in various ways. To do so is, in effect, giving up our right or ability to exercise free choice. We can voluntarily put ourselves in the hands of someone or something else. We do this when we board an airplane and take off for some distant place. The pilot and the air worthiness of the craft itself will determine what happens to us. There is little we can do about our own safety once airborne. When we step on an elevator to rise to a higher floor in a building, we place our safety on the integrity of the mechanical and electronic soundness of the equipment. These events are so commonplace that we hardly ever question it. We can't not do it if we are to gain the advantages of modern technology.

There is something different about our placing ourselves in the hands of some authoritarian leader, perhaps a charismatic one. People implicitly and blindly yielded their will to James Jones who in turn subjected his follows to mass suicide and murder.

We can also abdicate our responsibility when we become intoxicated with alcohol or other drugs. We render our minds inoperable with respect to making rational decisions. Free-will goes out the window. We place ourselves in the hands of fate or other people.

Presence of Psychiatric and Neurological Disorders

There are a host of psychiatric and neurological disorders that interfere with making unencumbered choices. The severest of them are dementia and psychosis. In the worst cases, one clearly cannot exercise free-will. Their origin is largely from neurological disease or physical trauma. The impairment can be continual or episodic. In the latter, when a crime is committed, courts often have a difficult time determining whether the criminal act is attenuated because of illness. Chapter VI goes further into problems about free choice. There we consider the underlying causes for apparently stupid acts that occur for reasons other than stupidity.

In the next chapter, Chapter IV, we take a look at a number of illustrations of behaviors we have commonly thought of as stupid.

CHAPTER *IV*

What are Some Behaviors We Have Labeled as Stupid?

Richard Milhous Nixon's Watergate Cover-up

On Friday, June 23, 1972, a week to the day from the time of the Watergate break-in, President Richard Milhous Nixon was conversing with H. R. (Bob) Haldeman, White House chief-of-staff. Haldeman informed the president that the FBI had linked the cash that was found on the Watergate burglars to the Committee to Re-Elect the President (CREEP, a curiously appropriate acronym). Knowing that this would bring the investigation to the very door of the White House, Haldeman suggested a solution. He wanted to trick the CIA into warning the FBI away from a crucial part of its inquiry. The proposal was clearly a lie and definitely illegal. Nixon's response as recorded three times on audio tapes was "all right fine" then concluding with "you call them in. Good. Good deal. Play it tough [pressuring those who were to intercede with the CIA]...."[35] Later in the day, Nixon elaborated on how the scheme could

---

[35] Summers, Anthony. The Arrogance of Power: the Secret World of Richard Nixon (New York: Viking, 2000). P. 432.

be accomplished. Recorded on tape was the smoking gun concerning Nixon's obstruction of justice. On Friday, August 9, 1974, Nixon resigned from the Office of President of the United States. Where was the fatal flaw in Nixon that brought him to this outcome?

Richard Nixon was born on January 9, 1913, the second boy among five sons born to Frank Nixon and Hannah Milhous. His place of birth was in a Sears, Roebuck house erected by his father on a twelve acre site destined to become a lemon grove.[36] Its location was in Yorba Linda, thirty miles outside of Los Angeles. Although Nixon enjoyed portraying himself as coming from humble origins (apparently wanting to attach himself to the lore of Abraham Lincoln), his family was regarded as firmly entrenched in the middle class. Richard's father was of Irish descent, of a character reflective of the stereotyped hard drinking, combative Irishman. Richard in later years, according to Summers, described his father as "a scrappy, belligerent fighter, with a quick, wide-ranging raw intellect....It was his temper that impressed me most as a small child....He was a strict and stern disciplinarian." Nixon's psychiatrist of forty years, Dr. Arnold Hutschnecker of New York City, said that "Nixon's father was brutal and cruel." A family friend defined Frank Nixon as a hard, beastly man, more like an animal. He made a reasonably good living as the owner/operator of a convenience store and service station.

Nixon's mother, Hannah, was one of nine children whose father was a well-to-do rancher. He and his wife were devout Quakers. When she was twenty-three she met twenty-seven year old Frank Nixon at a party and four months later married him. By her stepping outside the Quaker faith to choose a husband, she was for a time regarded as a rebel. Frank later converted to the Quaker religion.

Although Richard adopted some of his father's characteristics such as the tough demeanor, he internalized many of his mother's values. She was devout in her religion and had the family attending church four times

---

[36] *Ibid.* P. 1.

each Sunday. They never had a meal without saying grace. However, Hannah had a temper as well as her husband but she displayed it by conducting stern lectures designed to elicit guilt feelings. Her children dreaded her words more than they would spankings. Neighbors described her as "cranky and puritanical" and "hard…pure steel, pure steel."[37]

Hannah never had any hugs or kisses for anyone. She never said "I love you" to anyone including himself according to Nixon. Hannah did devote time to Richard in helping him with his studies. This usually meant long hours of homework. Richard never expressed resentment over this in later life. He was considered a brilliant student from an early age.

Summers[38] cites Nixon's psychiatrist as reporting Nixon to be "an emotionally deprived child." He goes on to say he "grew up to become a 'person who regarded love and physical closeness as a diversion that would drain him, deplete him, make him less manly. Love…never had priority in Nixon's life, for he always convinced himself that he didn't need to be loved as a human being, only respected as a man.'"

The key to Nixon's downfall according to Summers[39] was his lust for power. And true to the saying "power corrupts and absolute power corrupts absolutely" we have a path leading from power to corruption to deceit.

However, there is ample evidence that the pattern of deceitfulness began early in Nixon's childhood. Perhaps it began with the episode Nixon related to a close aide, here repeated as described by Summers. "One day…Hannah Nixon baked some cookies. Little Richard saw those cookies and ate one of them. And she said, 'Richard, did you eat that cookie?'" He didn't know any better than to say yes, and she beat the daylights out of him…." The aide surmised that it was a lifelong lesson to Nixon: it doesn't pay to tell the truth. Subsequently we see Nixon's propensity to engage in deceptions and outright lies. His high school debating coach

---

37 *Ibid.* P. 8.
38 *Ibid.* P. 9.
39 *Ibid.*

was distressed at Nixon's ability to "slide around an argument." One teacher noted that he had a mean way to get his point across. A neighbor commented that "he wouldn't hesitate to twist the truth." He secretly violated rules when competing on his Whittier College debate team.

A most revealing episode occurred while he was a law student at Duke University in North Carolina. The story was reported to a local newspaper writer in 1960. It was later boastfully confirmed by Nixon himself. While in his second year at Duke, he and two other students broke into the dean's office one night. It has always been unclear what their motive was because explanations varied. Nixon claimed credit for the break-in because as the thinnest of the three he was able to climb through the transom and unlock the door from within for the other two young men to gain entrance.

Nixon brought up the subject of robbing and undertaking break-ins while in office prior to the Watergate burglary. Summers cites a conversation that President Nixon held with White House counsel John Dean. Unhesitatingly Nixon remarked that they could break into his political enemy's office: "there are ways to do it….Goddamnit, sneak in in the middle of the night."

At various times in his career, even while campaigning for his first political office, Nixon said that he embraced a Machiavellian view of politics. He was quoted as saying dissembling and hypocrisy were necessary to win and hold public office. Summers quotes both Henry Kissinger and John Ehrlichman saying respectively: that Nixon was convinced that his distortion of fact was actually true fact and "I doubt if he knows himself when he's not telling the truth." This is a sign of a pathological liar. The former Chief Justice of the Supreme court, Earl Warren, thought Nixon to be "despicable…a cheat, a liar, and a crook…."[40]

Nixon's psychiatrist has commented that though Nixon was subject to periodic severe depressive episodes, he was not psychotic. He does,

---

[40] *Ibid.* P. 117.

however, state that he believed Nixon had a personality disorder attributed primarily to his mother's influence.

What was behind Nixon's lack of judgment that led to the big lie and the Watergate cover-up scandal? It was a matter of personality and character on a global scale. It was the sort of man he was. Summers[41] quotes Kissinger who commented that Nixon was "like a figure in Greek tragedy, he was fulfilling his own nature and destroying himself."

William Jefferson Clinton and Monica Levinsky

It was during the government shutdown on November 15, 1995 that twenty-two-year-old White House intern, Monica Lewinsky, discovered President Clinton alone in the office of Chief of Staff Leon Panetta. This was the first occasion that they were ever together without others' being present. They had never before spoken to one another. Monica had her mind set on seducing the President. With a cryptic expression on her face, she lifted her jacket above her waist giving the President a glance at her thong underwear.

Some hours later at 8 P.M., Monica chose to go to the bathroom that was closest to Clinton's offices. In doing so she passed by George Stephanopoulos' office where Clinton was alone. He noticed her and asked her to come in. He carried on with small talk but she stopped him by saying "You know, I have a really big crush on you." He immediately invited her to his private study and kissed her. They then parted but later the same evening he discovered her alone in Panetta's office and he led her "to the tiny hallway that ran from the closed door of Stephanopoulos's office to the closed door of the Oval Office....It was the only place in the White House where the president could pretty much guarantee that he

---

[41] *Ibid.* P. 452.

would not be seen by anyone."[42] It was an awkward place for a tryst, requiring a very willing partner. Monica was obliging.

At the point when Clinton "noticed" Monica for the second time that evening, he made a stupid blunder. His noticing was characterized by lust, a lust which he acted upon. The time between his first observing Monica's underwear and the time he saw her outside George's office, was a time that permitted Clinton's fantasies to percolate. There is nothing more conducive to sexual acting out than the arousal of sexual fantasies. This is especially so in one who is habituated to having promiscuous, adulterous encounters as he was. The sexual fantasy acts as a trigger to overt sexual activity.

President Clinton had made numerous blunders in his life both before and after his running for president in 1992. From the time Paula Jones made her accusations public, Clinton goofed in the handling of the press, the public, his family, the White House staff, and the whole chain of legal matters. But nothing could stand above the seriousness of his affair with Monica Lewinsky.

What were some of the things that made the Monica thing so stupid? Most of all were the exceedingly high odds that he would be caught and exposed. Though he swore Monica to keep their relationship secret, he later acknowledged to a confidant that he knew that she could not keep it to herself. Everyone was aware beyond a doubt that Clinton was intellectually brilliant. It did not take much to conclude that a twenty-two-year-old, naive woman would be tempted to relate to others that she was having a torrid sexual relationship with the President of the United States, the most powerful man in the world.

Could he justify in his own mind that his relationship with Monica was "a personal matter," one not in conflict with his oath of office? Perhaps he could. But could he reasonably expect a majority of others to excuse him on the grounds that it was his private life? No! This was especially so

---

[42] Toobin, Jeffrey. A Vast Conspiracy: The Real Story of the Sex Scandal that Nearly Brought Down a President (New York: Touchstone, 1999). P. 86.

because he was all too aware already that there was "a vast conspiracy" aligned against him. He had known for years that he had bitter enemies who wanted to destroy him personally and politically. Nearly twenty-one months prior to his meeting Monica, Paula Jones had announced to the world her charge about his sexual indiscretion regarding her. President Clinton was a target for scandal and he knew it.

Since his relationship with Monica was obviously consensual did that excuse it? First, it obviously didn't on the grounds of adultery. He admitted to wrong doing in this regard as well as regards to violating moral and religious principles. Second, there was the ethical issue of a middle aged man taking advantage of a woman who, with respect to age, could have been his daughter. Third, Monica was in an official subordinate role to him. A strict interpretation of sexual harassment law regarding the workplace makes *any* sexual relationship in a superior to subordinate role legally harassing. As a psychologist, psychotherapist, and mental health administrator, I had fully supported this strict interpretation. (Later, there was an easing in the application of the law to the workplace). A psychotherapist engaging in sex with one of his patients would be abridging the trust and contractual obligation he owed the patient. For the administrator, there would be a divestment of authority and discordance cast among other employees.

Fourth, what about judgment? The activities with Monica Lewinsky in Clinton's own mind would have raised a question about his judgment, not in just sexual matters but in all matters. It is true that people are capable of compartmentalizing their mental processing. They can keep aspects of their sexual behavior separate in their minds from international diplomacy, for example. However, the employment of logic tight compartments in one's mind in itself, is not indicative of a psychologically healthy individual.

Finally, as President of the United States he cannot be regarded as just any other man. The same standards cannot be afforded him as the ordinary citizen. His oath of office, though not specifically stated, should imply upholding the dignity of that office. Would the president of the

United States go uncensored if under normal circumstances he were to attend a state dinner with the president of a foreign nation dressed in a polo shirt and jeans?

I believe such an act would cause serious problems. This issue of dignity should apply to sexual indiscretions whether discovered or undiscovered. The preceding is aimed at describing the cardinal act of stupidity in the Clinton scandals. Next, is consideration of the why and how concerning this brilliant, highly knowledgeable, chief executive's stupid improprieties.

The search for an explanation of Clinton's behavior takes us into the realm of personality. For some years now, mental health experts, criminologists, and even historians have engaged in psychological profiling. This is an effort to describe the workings of an individual's mind without conducting direct formal diagnostic procedures or in some cases without ever seeing the individual or knowing his identity. The technique rests upon secondary sources of information such as official records about the person's behavior and personal history, anecdotal evidence from friends or acquaintances, the person's writings, etc. Obviously, the accuracy of the method is largely dependent upon the reliability and validity of the sources. The interpreter, even when given good data, must exercise extreme caution in drawing conclusions. Psychological profiling, though valuable, is extremely speculative.

Evaluating the personality of a politician to determine his suitability to serve in public office is legitimate. (Some psychiatrists have expressed the idea that candidates for the presidency should undergo formal mental health assessments prior to running for office. It's an idea that won't be implemented in the foreseeable future. One reason is because of the inexactitude of the psychological field). The procedure of the U.S. Senate's conducting "advice and consent" hearings on presidential appointments invariably touches on personality issues. A case in point is the recent hearings on the nomination of John Ashcroft to the office of U.S. attorney general. Unfortunately, such proceedings don't give personality evaluation the importance that it deserves. We have arrived at the point in our thinking that it is not enough to know a person by his public record alone. We are concerned about future performance and we know that with human beings there is no certain way of predicting subsequent behavior. To the extent that we can understand the thinking, motives, values, principles, and ideologies of a person—all inner mental processes—the better we feel about the vision we have of his future actions. Thus, people have addressed the question of what kind of man is Bill Clinton. I also will take a brief glimpse to help explain how this smart person did stupid things.

Among Clinton's principal enemies was a former friend, Cliff Jackson, of Arkansas.

Jackson met a kindred soul in 1992, a reporter then of *The Washington Post*, who held similar views of Clinton. The reporter was Michael Isikoff who referred to Clinton as a *sexual addict*.[43] Is this the explanation? Was or is Clinton a sexual addict?

Carnes[44] offers a description of sexual addiction when he describes the typical behavioral cycle of the sexual addict. He views it as a four-step process beginning with a period of *preoccupation*. The addict becomes obsessed with sexual fantasies which are usually specific to a preferred fixation. His (not all sexual addicts are male) mind is engrossed with the sexual ideas accompanied by a distinct change in mood. The mood is one of exquisite anticipation of impending sexual gratification. The preoccupation may be triggered by an intrusive thought or some stimulating event in the environment such as seeing an attractive woman. This state of mind is not far removed from normal experience. With the addict, however, there is a strong inclination to seek stimulation and to prolong the anticipatory aspect. With them it is a more insistent need.

Carnes next describes *ritualization* as the second addictive step. The addicted individual develops over time a specific pattern of behavior that is routinely followed. The routine or ritual is accompanied by the

43 *Ibid.* P. 33.

44 Carnes, Patrick. The Sexual Addiction (Minneapolis: CompCare Publications, 1983).

thoughts and mood already set in motion. Stage one and two together intensify the sexual arousal and excitement. They become as important and gratifying to the addict as the sexual act itself. The pattern ultimately leads to the next, culminating stage, the compulsive act.

The *compulsive sexual behavior*, writes Carnes, cannot be controlled or brought to a stop.

The fourth and final step is *despair*. The addict experiences a sense of hopelessness and powerlessness regarding his addiction. It leads to a painful sense of alienation. There is a distinct feeling that no one would ever understand him or forgive his behavior if it were revealed. Unfortunately, relief can be achieved by setting the cycle into motion again.

Certain other characteristics are determining in this addiction cycle. One is an absence of a fulfilling, sustained relationship with another human being. Another is the inability to manage one's life. The addictive cycle becomes the exclusive focus of one's being. One is unable to maintain normal responsibilities.

As Carnes points out not everyone having sexual problems is an addict. He gives a number of examples of non-addictive patterns of behavior that do not describe Clinton. However, Clinton is not a sexual addict if the above description is used as the defining criteria.

Bill Clinton is opportunistic in his sexual acting out. He is not a sexual predator. There is little if any planning and forethought to bring about his sexual encounters. He takes advantage of a situation when it occurs. He experiences the potential sexual partner as another human being and he values the fact that they will experience sexual fulfillment in any encounter they might have. He has feelings of mutuality and attachment although he recognizes the futility of trying to sustain an on-going affair with a particular partner. He wishes to spare his family pain if at all possible.

---

45 Fick, Paul. The Dysfunctional President: Understanding the Compulsions of Bill Clinton (Secaucus, NJ: Carol Publishing Group, 1998).

Clinton is not alienated from other people. He is, in fact, notably dependent upon and engaged in many non-sexual, interpersonal relationships. He is at the core trusting of other individuals and he can anticipate their understanding, acceptance, and forgiveness for his personal failings. He experiences the feelings of embarrassment, shame, and guilt. However, in general, his sexual escapades are rationalized as victimless indiscretions. The strength of his urges and the pleasure derived from their fulfillment justify the negative consequences of the great risk of discovery. His being able to get away with indiscretions over a period of years makes it easier to continue the pattern.

As important as sex is to Clinton, it does not push aside all other interests and endeavors. He is able to function exceedingly well in spite of his sexual proclivities. Sexual acting out does not control his life. Since the accusation has been made about Clinton being a sexual addict, it has been important to discount it as an explanation for the stupid Monica Lewinsky episode.

Another theory put forth about Clinton's personality needs to be explored. During the first two years of Clinton's first term, a clinical psychologist by the name of Paul Fick wrote a book whose general thesis was that Clinton was psychologically unfit to be president. The book was replete with rumor, half-truths, speculations, and out-right lies but it's assertion that Clinton was reared with an alcoholic, surrogate father is true. Fick writes that Clinton himself admits to being an adult child of an alcoholic (ACOA).

Research on ACOA as a condition suggests that caution must be used because not everyone reared by an alcoholic parent or parents will manifest a negative pattern of behavior. Some seem to benefit from the experience. Various personal characteristics attributed to the ACOA may not be distinguishable from those in the general population. Conclusions must be considered tentative and the identification of this condition is likely to be the total configuration of a number of traits.

Some characteristics attributed to ACOA are low self-esteem, distrust of one's own feelings, avoidance of conflict, need to be a peacemaker, dissembling, approval seeking, need for achievement, perfectionism, need for control of others, over sensitivity to criticism, explosive temper, inclined to sabotage oneself, and difficulties in regulating sexual drives. To apply any of these particular traits to Clinton is somewhat like getting a psychic reading from a stranger over the telephone. One must be cautious. If any of these are significant, what stands out to me is Clinton's drive for success, his need to be a peacemaker, becoming the personality kid, wanting control, and having problems with sex. The latter, I believe, is perhaps secondary to his seeking acceptance and wanting to be affirmed as an lovable individual.

The Two Ex-Presidents Compared

It is a most amazing coincidence that we have had two presidents in recent years who have either faced or undergone impeachment who share a fundamental psychological problem. The two men are of course, Richard Milhous Nixon and William Jefferson Clinton. Sexual dysfunction has played a commanding role in both of their lives. With Clinton it is obvious. With Nixon it is covert. I have previously addressed Nixon's problems but not the underlying sexual dynamic, nor have I yet delved into the depth of Clinton's sexual problem from a psychological perspective. I do that now and subsequently pull together the comparison of the two former presidents.

Clinton was born in a small town in Arkansas in 1946. His biological father, William Jefferson Blythe, III, was killed in an automobile accident while his mother, Virginia Cassidy Blythe, was six months pregnant. While Virginia was in pursuit of a degree as a nurse anesthetist in New Orleans, she placed Bill in the custody of her parents in Hope, Arkansas. When Bill was four years of age, his mother married Roger Clinton. The family moved to Hot Springs. By the time Bill was eight years of age, his stepfather's drinking got out of hand and there were many arguments, wife battering, and physical abuse of the children. Bill's mother divorced Roger when Bill was fourteen but she remarried Roger three months later. Then at his mother's request, Bill changed his last name to Clinton.

It was reported that Bill, at an early age, tried to intercede in his parent's battles. He was protective of his mother and younger half-brother, Roger. He called the police on one occasion that resulted in his father's arrest. When Bill was fifteen years old, it has been said, Bill confronted his drunken step-dad and thus put an end to the physical violence.

Both Bill and his mother regarded Roger as a good man except when he was drunk. They admit to having affection for him. While Bill was attending law school at Georgetown University in Washington, D. C. his stepfather died.

Although Clinton grew up in a very dysfunctional family, his relationship with his mother and grandparents provided him with an atmosphere of unconditional love. The Clinton's were affectionate, demonstrative people. His mother stood by him as best she could. She took an intense interest in his success from his earliest years. The conflict between his mother and stepfather brought mother and son closer together since an alliance was necessary to protect themselves from irreversible harm. They also needed to hold their heads high to counteract the shame and humiliation of Roger's alcoholism. Bill expressed great respect, admiration, and affection for his mother. He admired her for her intelligence, accomplishments as a professional, and devotion to the family.

As is typical of a child in an alcoholic family, Bill spent as much time away from home as he could. Much of it was in the homes of relatives, friends, and neighbors. It was to his advantage to be a cordial, polite, friendly guest not to wear out his welcome. These circumstances probably contributed greatly to his being people oriented. Approval and affirmation from others served to bolster his bruised self-esteem. Being an exceedingly bright student, a high achiever, and popular, made him an attractive target for girls.

Clinton's active sexual life as an adult suggests his having lost his virginity at an early age. Early shared sexual intimacy typically leads to hypersexuality in adult life. Bill became fixated on heterosexual relationship at the time his testosterone levels were running rampant. There's little doubt that he was naturally more endowed with respect to hormones than the average male. Also, in the words of Henry Kissinger, power is the ultimate aphrodisiac; and political success, whether as president of a high school class or of the United States, signals power. The free love ethic of the sixties also lowered the threshold for a teenager to become sexually active. He probably relished the thrill of illicit sex. The pursuit and conquest theme can be bolstering to the ego. Thus, in Clinton's adult life, his habitual pattern of seeking sexual gratification overcame his reason to the point that he got caught.

Richard Nixon's early childhood and adolescence are in stark contrast to Clinton's. Also, in stark contrast was his sexual history. What was common in the two men's lives was the dominant role their respective mother's played in their psychosexual development. Nixon's mother was emotionally cold and unexpressive. She never said "I love you" to anyone in her adult life as far as is known. She gave a great deal of personal attention to Nixon, particularly with respect to his academic studies, but an overt expression of affection was non-existent between them. This is how Nixon remembered her. Nixon was regarded by girls during his youth as being a bore and non-sexy. He remained a virgin until married at the age of twenty-seven. His marriage with Pat was rife with tension and there was never any public display of affection between them. Instead, there were numerous incidents in which he treated her coldly and rudely. Even when president of the United States, jokes were common about Nixon being asexual. One in particular concerned his "semi-annual erection which he relieved on trips to Havana."[46]

---

[46] *Op Cite.* Summers.

The mothers of the two men were regarded by them as central in importance in their lives. Each had their mothers placed on the proverbial pedestal. The mothers were over-idealized but in a totally different way. Clinton's mother spoke to his Yin and Nixon's to his Yang. As a result, Clinton is often seen as soft and feminine (and is disliked by a majority of men); whereas, Nixon was known to be hard, often cruel, and manfully authoritarian.

Choosing of Political Leaders

These two recent presidents had made extraordinarily stupid mistakes during their respective administrations. People in this country and many throughout the world were shaking their heads in amazement and puzzlement when the critical facts were revealed. The American people expect the elected president of the United States to perform his duties to the best of his ability, putting the interests of its citizens before all others. They expect that he would have ability beyond those of ordinary men. They expect that he would have personality characteristics that are prerequisite to an able job performance. These would include even temperament, mental as well as physical stamina, moral courage, ethical values, foresight, and so on. Since in today's political system presidential candidates are primarily career politicians who have worked their way through the ranks of various political offices, we must realize that any political position demands careful scrutiny of its candidates. They must be evaluated as to intellectual ability, administrative competence, character, and personal integrity. These traits must be examined whether it is for the position of PTA president as in the case of Spiro Agnew, city council, mayor, states attorney, governor, congressman, or senator. Little do we realize that in the act of electing a president of our high school class or community association we may be launching the career of a future U.S. President. It is a fact that one's vote is more meaningful at the grassroots level (in local elections) than in any other political event. We all too commonly make mistakes we later regret when voting for a political candidate. They are often stupid mistakes. Some are described in detail when discussing reasons in Chapter V. We now move on to some other behaviors that society is inclined to label as stupid.

Risk Takers

Generally speaking, I'm not a risk taker nor was my father. I probably followed in his footsteps. A major influence on him was reaching young adulthood in the early twenties when ordinary men had a difficult time obtaining jobs (contrary to the myth that "the roaring twenties" represented the "good times"). This was greatly magnified by the onset of the Great Depression at the end of the decade and most of the next. Getting a secure job and holding it ran counter to the taking of risks.

However, as a child and in my youth I knew what it was to take risks. I was all too ready to do stupid things on a dare from my playmates. I'm lucky not to have died from poisons or been killed by falling from a cliff or having the roof of a cave collapse upon me. Three things seemed to drive me on those occasions. One was to impress my friends. Two was to bolster my own ego. And the third was an insatiable curiosity. In nearly every instance there was no prospect of material gain.

My scaling of rock cliffs was done during my preteens, unsupervised and without any special equipment. Although the rock walls I undertook to climb were of modest difficulty, they were high enough that a fall could have easily resulted in serious injury or death. As I reflect upon my state of mind at the time, I believe the Edmund Hillary observation about mountain climbing applied to me. His remark following the conquest of Everest in 1953 was something to the effect "I did it because it was there." Ascending a cliff is simply a challenge. A little voice inside says "I want to prove that I can do it." It's an exercise in affirming one's athleticism, determination, and courage. There was no glory to be obtained since, at most, a few friends would be there to observe.

As an adult, the closest thing that came to these childhood experiences was solo sailing. When sailing alone on a large expanse of water, I experienced a combined sense of humility and awe. There is a feeling of mastery when thinking about being able to get where you want to go simply be manipulating sails and rudder. In theory, I could sail to nearly anywhere on earth. Though practically speaking it was impossible, the fantasy was deliciously real.

The sailor is reduced to three basic elements: the boat and its sails; the water and weather; and himself. There is little one can do about the water and the weather, hence, the risk. There is a sense of being on the edge. One is engaging in calculated risk. The risk is reduced by having taken proper care of your boat, having life jackets aboard, being in a good state of mind and health, having signaling and electronic communications, keeping up-to-date navigational charts, and keeping abreast of the latest weather reports.

If I were to get in trouble in my sailing, I'm sure the U.S. Coast Guard and others would say that I had acted stupidly. Why take such a risk people would ask. My decision was based on assessing the odds of failure against those of the rewards of success.

Here is where the rub is. There are those who go beyond rational limits. Instead of being risk takers they are reckless daredevils. Most anything that is accomplished in society involves some degree of risk. When we undertake doing something that appears chancy, we need to assess the risk/benefit ratio. Part of this calls for the examination of motives. Why am I contemplating doing this? Is it primarily to get attention ? Is it to gain some immediate but fleeting gratification? Is it for excitement? Is it to prove something to myself such as having heroic traits? Is it to protect the life of someone else? Is it to accomplish some greater social good? Risking one's life to save another when one's perception is that there is some glimmer of the possibility of success is a rational act. To attempt a leap across a deep crevice just to see if you can make it to the other side is stupid.

What we choose to do may be clearly a dangerous undertaking. Challenging sports offer examples of high risk activities. Skydiving, mountain climbing, Alpine skiing, white water kayaking, solo sailing, bungy jumping are a few examples. Those who pursue such sports are not stupid. Those who engage in high risk sports without proper training and without making reasonable effort to reduce known risks are stupid. Smart skydivers pack their own parachutes. Smart whitewater kayakers wear helmets and life jackets and always take a partner with them. Smart Alpine skiers keep an eye on the weather, heed avalanche warnings, and always take a partner with them. I move on to other kinds of behaviors we would generally deem to be stupid.

Doomed Marriages

The high prevalence of divorce in our society may be measured by its simple dramatic increase since the end of WWII. Today, a marriage has one chance in two of ending in divorce. The high risk year is the first and it gradually trails off in frequency as the years together progress. Needless to say there are innumerable reasons for divorce to occur and many reasons for explaining the dramatic increase over the past fifty years. Society has changed significantly, especially as measured by the differences in roles that women now hold compared to their grandmothers. The family has and is being subjected to enormous social, economic, cultural, and ideological pressures.

Many professionals devoted to the study of marriage maintain that divorce is not an altogether bad thing. Where there is significant incompatibility that cannot be resolved then divorce seems to be the logical outcome. The extremes of behavioral disturbance such as spouse abuse, persistent infidelity, and other un-ameliorated personality and character disorders in one or both spouses usually lead to the dissolution of a marriage. Well they should. Children, whether teenage or younger, may be better off with their argumentative and combative parents living apart. Even when things are not as severe as just noted divorce may be a rational solution. One partner in the marriage may feel compelled to go his or her own way because of differences in values, life style, or career choice. This could happen conceivably when the couple still felt love for one another.

However one looks at it, though, the process of divorce is usually extremely emotionally painful and seriously disruptive in many practical ways. (The rather frequent pattern of committed cohabitation without a marriage ceremony and public record does not lessen substantially the agony of a break-up). If one is concerned about his or her well being, then the act of marriage should be given utmost consideration.

The fact that a major portion of marriages end within the first years following the ceremony supports the conclusion that many marriages never should have occurred in the first place. In such cases the proposition is well supported that there was a basic incompatibility during courtship. Proceeding from the courtship phase to marriage may be an example of stupidity. Of course, there are many marriages that survive the early years simply because the couple "sticks it out." Finally, they may reach a point years later when one or the other bails out. These also may have been doomed marriages that should have been foreseen before a long term commitment was made.

Here are a few examples where obvious warning signals exclaiming "go no further in this relationship" are commonly disregarded. Over-possessiveness in a partner usually accompanied by extreme jealousy should not be interpreted as a strong commitment or compliment to oneself. See it for what it is. It is an indicator in the suitor of deep insecurity, a need to be controlling, and of having the potential for subsequent physical abuse in the relationship. Persons who show this behavior during courtship commonly do not engage other individuals or couples in dating activities, such as in double dating. They object to their partner having other friends even when they are long-time, same sexed "buddies." They make all the decisions with little regard to their partner's wishes or needs.

Beware of the partner who reaches the point of expecting a commitment to marriage who has had the opportunity to introduce the other to his or her family and hasn't. Similarly, if the person hasn't introduced his partner to other friends and associates extreme caution is advised. Someone who acts mysteriously about his or her personal past life may be hiding something very meaningful that could later sabotage the relationship. A stricture against "no secrets" at all between one another is not mandatory, but a general openness to sharing one's past should be a prerequisite to remaining companionable.

Needless to say, one's antennae should go up when a partner displays excessive use of intoxicants, irresponsibility in money management, extreme moodiness, spells of reclusiveness, hyper-criticism of others, frequent lying, and explosive temper, especially if it reaches the point of rage. Any of these suggest the likelihood of a looser. Marriage to one showing habituation to these traits is an indication of stupidity.

Rage Reactions and Bad Temper in General

A number of individuals who engage in frequent outbursts of anger are likely to be displaying their stupidity. (Chapter V describes those showing excessive anger who are not stupid). The expression of anger can range from mild to uncontrollable rage. It will vary from person to person as to what triggers the reaction. For some, the cause may be what to others is a mild frustration or provocation. For others who respond with anger, observers may acknowledge that the triggering stimulus was of major proportions. In any case, overt anger is usually perceived as ugly, oftentimes frightening and dangerous. It seems to signal that the individual cannot handle a situation in a rational way. Irrationality can be scary. Anger seldom solves a problem. It usually creates more problems either immediately or sometime later.

Human infants and toddlers are expected to display temper tantrums. We would regard such expressions of anger, up to a point, as being normal. We see them as a manifestation of the young child's frustration over an inability to express himself in words so as to fulfill his needs. Custodial adults have growth enhancing ways of resolving the child's demands even when the specific need may be beyond the possibility of gratification. Also, the caring adult can steer the child toward employing crying to signal his needs rather than a full-blown, out-of-control tantrum. Unfortunately, there are adults who resort to temper tantrums either because they never gave them up or they regress to an infantile developmental level.

Speaking of children, we find that we have a problem regarding corporal punishment of children ranging from spanking to serious child abuse. Such actions against children are usually the result of parental frustrations that prompt loss of control and the overt expression of anger. The act of inflicting physical punishment may give a parent temporary release from tension and it is this that may be the prime motivator for its persistence. Because spanking often stops any ongoing action of the child it is viewed by some as useful. The child learns some or all of the following when spanked. Adults can and will hurt you. They are more powerful than you. They cannot always be trusted. They are not consistent in their love. Hitting or striking others is a legitimate means for releasing tension. It is a preferred way of dealing with conflict. The child experiences himself as "bad," usually not knowing precisely why in his own mind because the punishment is not connected clearly with any particular behavioral act on his part. In time, the child understands how to provoke the parent. The child gains some power over the parent by engaging in provocative behavior. The child may find that receiving negative attention is rewarding. A vicious cycle may ensue.

Spouse abuse is very common according to various surveys and crime statistics. It has been said that one in four women have experienced physical abuse from their husbands. Such behavior cannot be justified. It is immoral, illegal and stupid.

Much is being made of road rage these days. We frequently read in newspapers or see on TV incidents of someone killing another because of a simple driving incident. A recent local news article carried a story about an attack on a forty-eight-year-old construction worker who was directing traffic at the work site. A thirty-three year old man driving a pick-up truck attempted to pull around the line of backed up cars. The construction worker stepped in front of the pick-up to cause it to a stop. The driver got out of the vehicle, struck the worker in the face with his fist, and then proceeded to kick him repeatedly as he lay on the ground. Among the various injuries sustained by the worker was a crushed eye socket. Whether or not he will loose his sight is not yet known. The assailant drove off but was apprehended two days later. When caught it was learned that he had bragged to his boss about the altercation. He expressed no remorse. There's no justification for road rage and certainly it is not smart.

When I started out in my professional work, it was a common myth that one should not suppress his anger. Psychoanalytic theory even suggested that anger held in would lead to depression. A frequent metaphor that was cited referred to a boiling tea kettle on a hot stove. When the steam pressure built up within the pot, the steam would be released through the spout, resulting in a whistling noise (analogous to angry shouting). If the kettle had no open spout, it would explode. The implication was that anger was like that.

My experience with patients soon led me to see that the metaphor lacked a significant construct. In the case of the boiling tea kettle, one of two things should be done. One, the heat under the kettle should be turned down, or two, it should be shut off. Medical research is now suggesting that the experience of anger leads to a greater incidence of heart disease. Each of the various incidents cited above show that uncontrolled temper outbursts are potentially dangerous and are evidence of stupidity.

Crowd Disorder

We see bottle throwing from some fan in a crowd of spectators at sporting events. Passion we can understand and accept but such violent acts are inexcusable. The infectious nature of a crowd's response and the anonymity afforded by a large gathering doesn't justify violence. The individual who fuses his identity with a crowd mentality is acting stupidly.

When about the age of four, I was the unfortunate witness of an orgy of violence conducted by a group of older boys. It occurred in a wooded area near my home. For some reason or other there were a large number of box turtles collected on the ground. Probably some boys had gathered the turtles from the immediate surrounding area on a hunting and discovery venture. Abruptly, for no apparent reason, the boys started smashing and crushing the turtles until all were dead. Even though so young, I was aware of witnessing the intoxicating frenzy and contagious expenditure of energy that was associated with the debauchery. It was as though the Freudian death drive was suddenly unleashed in that group of boys.

Strangely enough, I related that childhood incident to the Vietnam, My Lai atrocity that occurred in 1968. Troops of the American Eleventh Infantry Brigade beat, raped, fired upon, bayoneted to death, and burned over 350 defenseless Vietnamese civilians. Among the victims were the elderly of both sexes, women, children, and infants. The Americans had met no hostile fire on the day of the rampage. The only justification for initiating the violence had been a vague notion of an order "to waste them." One common element between the turtles of my childhood and the villagers was that both were innocent living creatures, not deserving of a senseless, cruel, violent death. Another common element was the contagious destructiveness of the perpetrators. Not one among the many soldiers or their officers in the initial group acted autonomously. None made an effort to assert his individuality and demand a stop to the madness.

Ideological Extremes

In the middle 1960's, I was engaged in private practice (psychological services) from an office in downtown Baltimore. The building in which my office was situated was formerly a large, four story town home. Most of the old houses in the immediate vicinity were either converted offices or apartment buildings. Diagonally across the street and in easy view of my office window was a building housing a substantial number of members of the *hare krishnas*. They were all young men with shaven heads, beads, and white robes. They frequently stood on the street beating tambourines, singing, and begging for money. This was my first close encounter with members of a cult. My thoughts about them were that they were wasting away their lives. I was sure that they had good intelligence and talents. Given hair and conventional clothes, they would look like typical college students and even young, assistant college professors. I had uncomfortable feelings about them ranging from embarrassment to disgust. I had no fear of them but I preferred to avoid all close encounters.

This was the beginning of the period when parents of cult members hired detectives to locate and kidnap their teenage and young adult children from cults that had lured them into membership. It was a controversial procedure because of its coerciveness and illegality, particularly with respect to the violations of civil liberties. Some critics likened the cults to early Christianity and saw no harm in them. The kidnappings led to a career of deprogrammers whose task it was to rid the former members from the brainwashing they had undergone. Some were successful and some were not. Success was usually measured by the young person's gratitude at returning to the life of his pre-cult experience.

When thinking about cults along the lines of the *hare krishnas*, I categorically have regarded them as evil. To the extent that their recruitment and retention of members involved deception and duress, I was and remain convinced that I am correct in my assessment. However, in the absence of deviousness I'm not convinced that all such groups are destructive. There is a long history of utopian groups in America going back to the 1680's.[47] Their creation was variously motivated along such lines as political, social, economic, or religious leanings. They tended toward simplicity in all things. They were small in numbers and strove to be self-sufficient. Most originated with a charismatic leader and the only compulsion to join may have been at the hands of the head of a household.

There are definitions of the word "cult" within the dictionary that have benign meaning. An example is the allusion to such a thing as "the physical fitness cult." The particular meaning that goes as follows is the meaning I employ: "[The cult is] a religion or sect considered to be false, unorthodox, or extremist, with members often living outside conventional society under the direction of a charismatic leader." I must grant that there are marginal groups along the line as defined above. The determination as to value lies with the wisdom of conventional society. Those cults that employ coercion upon its followers and engage in illegal acts such as theft, child abuse, and murder within and outside the group are clearly of evil character. Being involved in one may be regarded as stupid.

Such groups labeled as survivalists, militias, and ideological extremists are similar in many ways to destructive cults. To their credit, there is usually less deception and coercion in obtaining recruits. Membership is usually voluntary. It comes about by drawing like-minded individuals together by invitation. Once a member, however, devious means are often employed to keep individuals within the fold. There is most often a heavy propaganda effort by these groups to gain recognition, define identity, and acquire new members.

In the mid 1970's, one of my patients was a young female student from a local community college. She was the daughter of a preacher and she had become incorrigible in her adolescent rebelliousness. She began discussing a

---

[47] Holloway, Mark. Heavens on Earth: Utopian Communities in America: 1680-1880 (New York: Dover Publications, Inc., 1966) and Hinds, William Alfred. American Communities (New York: Corinth Books, Inc. 1961 [reprinted from 1879]).

boyfriend from school who was engaging in some vicious fights on campus. She referred to him as being a "skin head." She told me, of course, that the phrase referred to the fact that they shaved their heads. I had not heard of them before and my immediate reaction was that it sounded like a lot of silliness. However, as she continued to describe them it became evident that they were a neo-Nazi group. I was then very, very concerned. College students are by definition regarded as intelligent and joining such a radical group would seem inconsistent. However, I was reminded of pre-Nazi Germany. The country was regarded as being at the pinnacle of artistic, technological, and intellectual accomplishment. Nevertheless, the German people allowed Adolph Hitler to seize and retain power. Clearly intelligence alone would not protect against stupid individual or collective actions.

This raises the question whether or not there is such a thing as collective stupidity. Putting it another way, is there such a thing as a group mind? If we think in terms of reification—making it concrete—the answer is "no." Functionally, however, there is group mind and the possibility of collective stupidity. Why? Groups are by definition a collective based on some shared traits or interests. It boils down to group members adhering to and supporting the defining characteristics of the group to which they belong. If individuals espouse stupid ideas and actions that form the basis of their belonging to a particular group then they contribute to the group dynamic.

We are confronted by a number of destructive or potentially destructive ideological groups such as the neo-Nazi, survivalist, and militia groups referred to above. We can add to that number various quasi-religious organizations and some fundamentalist sects. Also, included are some political organizations and other secular groups. According to Berlet and Lyons[48] it is a mistake to label these as a "lunatic fringe" or "marginal

---

[48] Berlet, Chip and Lyons, Matthew N. Right-Wing Populism in America: Too Close for Comfort (New York: The Guilford Press, 2000). P. 3.

'extremists.'" They are "…dangerous not because they are crazy irrational zealots—but because they are not." These authors comment how we find these people among our neighbors and in our work places. We see them as intelligent and well educated. They don't fit our common perception of an irrational, out-of-control person. That *is* what is most disturbing. They have many of our own "good," constructive, and humanitarian traits. They also have our negative or potentially negative characteristics. They thus threaten us at a deep psychological level as well as in some objective ways such as blowing up the neighborhood family planning clinic.

Among the distinguishing characteristics of these destructive organizations enumerated by Berlet and Lyons,[49] are the processes of dehumanizing, demonizing, scapegoating, conspiracizing, and Apocalyptic thinking. These were considered in detail in chapter II. The destructive and sometimes murderous goals and grandiose schemes along with the above mentioned characteristics render membership in such groups as stupid behavior. Why such choices are made by seemingly rational people is explored in the next chapter.

---

[49] *Ibid.* Pp. 6-13.

CHAPTER V

Why So Much Stupidity Among Smart People?

The question "why" though often asked is probably one of the most diffi-cult there is to answer. Usually, it directs us to examine motives which, of course, are subjective. Even if one were himself willing to offer an expla-nation as to why he behaved in a certain way and not another, we might very well doubt him. Our doubts would be based on such ideas that he may be lying to us, he may be trying to justify himself in his own mind, or he may have little or no grasp of the inner workings of his mind.

However, we can make inferences about motives based on observable behavior, including actions, verbalizations, and a wide range of non-verbal communications. We can do this with an individual regarding a single occasion or on multiple occasions over time. We also can observe a large number of people rather than a single person functioning in a common situation. We can assess their responses and in a way average them or form generalizations. We can negate observer bias to some extent by employing multiple, disinterested observers. We are thus approaching scientific research methodology.

Observing human behavior by other human beings has been going on since the first Homo Sapiens looked at themselves and their co-existing

94 • *Why Smart People Do Stupid Things*

hominid cousins. Their observations and conclusions were remembered and passed on to subsequent generations. In time, writing emerged and information passed onward without the risk of failures in memory.

These observations and conclusions had survival value. Once a "why" could be formulated concerning another's actions, it was possible to anticipate certain likely responses. For example, when the cave dweller stood up from the fire, he had a menacing look about him. The one approaching was alerted to the need to put the other at ease or be prepared to attack or defend himself. Here's another example. When the telemarketer says to us "we are sending you this absolutely free gift with no obligations attached," we go into our alert mode.

When assessing the why of our's and other's behavior, we have a vast reservoir of collected data upon which to base judgements.

Problems in Linguistics

The understanding of some sources of errors in reasoning and judgment may be found within the field of linguistics. This word in its broadest meaning pertains to language. Our language consisting of words and sentences works inside our minds as well as functions as the social tool of communication with others. Language is the bases of our ability to form ideas, to remember them, to organize them into complex notions, to engage in that mysterious process called reasoning, to give direction to our actions, and to communicate with others.

The science of linguistics traditionally has been divided into three categories. They are syntactics, semantics, and pragmatics. Although I will deal with them separately, it must be kept in mind that the boundaries between them are not precisely delineated. (The triadic division is based logically on its part to whole features. Syntactics is easiest to differentiate because it is formalistic and applies to structure. Semantics and pragmatics offer a problem since both deal with meaning. In the former, meaning is more specific where there is a closer link between language elements and their referents. The latter relates to meaning in a broader sense in which context, emotional, and other psychological components are taken into account). Within each there is the possibility for miscues that lead to incorrect, inaccurate, and fuzzy thinking. Consequently, such thoughts may lead to stupid utterances and actions. Thus it is important to gain some understanding of possible linguistic errors and find ways of correcting them.

Syntactics is all the rules pertaining to the formation of grammatical sentences in a language. By grammatical we mean sounds, morphemes (smaller elements that make up words such as "ed."), words, and sentence structure. Needless to say, syntactical rules as well as the other aspects of linguistics vary from one language to another. Anyone who studies a foreign language will soon discover that the rules of grammar differ, oftentimes in a confusing manner for us speakers of English. In fact, the very presence of a syntactical system defines a language.

Over a half a century ago, Wendell Johnson[50], a psychologist and semanticist, alluded to grammar, the structure of language, as the invention of man. The implication was that our language form is arbitrary. With respect to the invention of grammar, Johnson was correct. We owe our basic analysis of sentence structure to Aristotle (384-322 B.C.E.) who identified (or discovered) subject and predicate. He was followed by his countryman Dionysius Thrax (circa 150 B.C.E.) who gave us the parts of speech (specifically nouns, verbs, articles, pronouns, prepositions, conjunctions, adverbs, and participles). In the eighteenth century, English colonists discovered Sanskrit in India. In doing so, they recognized that a much more refined grammar had been worked out for this language over a period of three thousand years. The grammar was systematized by a Hindu named Panini circa 500 B.C.E. There is sufficient commonality between Sanskrit and our Western languages to make this grammar highly relevant.

---

[50] Johnson, Wendell. People in Quandaries (New York: Harper & Brothers, 1946).

The brief history does not, however, confirm Johnson's assumption of arbitrariness in the structure of our language. In the mid 1950's along came the mathematician and linguist, Noam Chomsky, of the Massachusetts Institute of Technology. He revolutionized the field of linguistics and advocated the belief that our propensity for structuring language as we do is inherent. It is, says Chomsky, a matter of genetics. Since then, there has been convincing scientific evidence to bear him out.

All syntactical errors are not a matter of genetic mutations, however. As useful and necessary (and apparently inevitably) the structure of language is, there is a built in slippery slope that leads to errors in reasoning and speaking.

Taking the word "smart" from this book's title, I can construct a simple sentence: "Jones is smart." The sentence consists of the three grammatical elements of a noun (subject), adjective, and verb (predicate). The noun designates a thing of some sort, in this instance a person named Jones. The adjective offers a quality pertaining to Jones. The verb shows the relationship between the other two parts of speech, in this instance inclusion or possession.

Johnson[51] following a similar example states: "This sort of language structure implies that reality is made up of things that possess qualities…colors, shapes, odors—*belong to things.*" The problem is that reality does not consist simply of things with attributes. There are, for example, space-time order and the relationship between the observer and the observed. Speaking of Jones as smart, we must consider the space-time dimension. Jones may not have always been "smart," and he may not be smart in every situation. Also, smartness is a quality that I attribute to Jones. It says something about me and my perception and definition of smartness.

As simplistic as this may seem, it nevertheless is a common source of error in our thinking and decision making. Rather than smartness, we might be talking about "stupid" or "nurd." Such words as all words carry

---

[51] *Ibid.* P. 121.

an emotional loading that shapes our opinions and affects our behavior. Through this analysis of syntactics we touch upon pragmatics.

One frequent way we make a word plural in English is to add the letter "s." This falls within the category of syntactics. It can make a difference in our understanding. For example, we might speak emphatically of "the *cause* of something." Might we not better refer to one of many possible cause(*s*). By leaving off an "s", we might go about many things in an over-determined manner.

Other grammatical errors and habits of speech (and thinking or lack thereof) include omissions that might be tagged by the speaker as "you know," implying that the listener is to fill in the blanks. The speaker typically hurries on to another train of thought. Well, the listener may not know and it may be ridiculous to expect that he would. Confusion may follow and probably the credibility of the speaker would be in question. An old, family, lady friend used to end nearly every spoken sentence with the phrase "don'cha know." It made listeners cringe in anticipation of hearing it. It also raised the question, if we already knew it why are you saying it?

Omissions are more serious in nature when they attain the status of ellipsis as understood in psychiatry. This is where the omission consisting of one or more words is done in an unconscious fashion. What is left out is something that the individual's conscious mind will not permit him to utter. To anyone other than the person's psychoanalyst, it would be very puzzling.

Still more serious is the occurrence of contaminations in one's communication. This is where one word is amalgamated with another. In a sense, a new word is created (neologism) and it is typically characteristic of psychosis.

There are varying forms of unintelligible incoherencies usually associated with one or another type of dementia. Some such behavior is described as "word salad." It consists of a mixture of words and phrases that are totally meaningless to the listener. In schizophrenia, it may be that a therapist can decode the messages with the patient's assistance.

Incoherence can reach the stage of babbling in which the speaker is unaware of not communicating meaningfully. This is usually indicative of advance stages of brain disease.

Semantics involves the study of why the combinations of certain words and sentences leads to meaning while other combinations do not. The human ability to obtain meaning from specific groupings of words may depend also upon the context in which they occur. (It is in the latter respect that blurring occurs with pragmatics).

A most insightful analogy regarding semantics was given by Korzybski.[52] It states simply that "a map is not the territory." He was speaking of *verbal* maps purporting to be reality. A verbal map is a kind of picture of the territory and one that oftentimes doesn't even come close to photographic accuracy. The verbal map consisting of words alone or those in some meaningful combination are not the things in themselves, the things they are a referent to. Words are a kind of symbol that represent some observable or unobservable (conjectured) aspect of reality. Our memories are a collection of verbal maps.

This phenomena can be illustrated by an old boardinghouse trick. When the diner at the end of the table asks for the pitcher of milk to be passed to him, without his knowledge an empty pitcher is slid across the table. As he goes to pick the pitcher up, he has in his mind the image of a vessel containing milk. He exerts a force he judges to be equal to the task and everyone laughs as his hand, arm, and empty pitcher leaps head high off the table.

It was not a joking matter when as a child I surmised that the black widow spider setting on an old washing machine, lacking movement, was dead. I picked it up and it was not.

Another example that also could have deadly consequences, is to arrive in your car at a fork in the road where the right turn has a barrier reading

---

[52] Korzybski, Alfred. Science and Sanity: An Introduction to Non-Aristotelian Systems and General Semantics (Lancaster: Science Press, 2nd Edition, 1941).

"road closed." Naturally, you either go to the left or turn around. Unknown to you, some prankster moved the sign from the left to the right. Your changing direction is an understandable error since we commonly take things on "authority."

Our words are abstractions and generalizations. If we are to live sanely we can't lose sight of that fact and we can't lose hold on the source and the chain of levels that abstractions and generalizations emerged from and went through. We need to retain the habit of obtaining first hand knowledge. Check it out! Obey the wisdom of the old saying "I'm from Missouri—you've got to show me." Keyes[53] identifies those who rely on second hand maps as having "parasitic minds."

Various principles that govern rational thought evolve from this basic concept regarding mapping the territory and levels of abstraction.[54]

One is a principle involving non-identity. No two things are ever *exactly* alike. A corollary is that no one person knows everything about anything. We cannot have complete verbal maps of the territory. We can only hope to have adequate ones. A consequence of this notion is that one should maintain an open mind. New ideas should be given a chance. One should attempt to gain as full a picture as possible before making judgements. Not doing so is to risk replicating the past in the face of a changing reality. When a person is making an assertion, he would be on safer ground by prefacing it with such phrases as "in my opinion," "as far as I know," and "I think." This leaves the channel open for other, perhaps differing opinions.

A second principle is that of non-absolutes. Most of reality presents itself on a continuum that must be marked and labeled by a series of degrees. This is commonly referred to as seeing shades of gray rather than

---

[53] Keyes, Kenneth S. Jr. How to Develop Your Thinking Ability (New York: McGraw-Hill Book Company, Inc., 1950). P. 29.

[54] Credit for this analysis must be given to Johnson, Wendell. People in Quandaries (New York: Harper & Brothers Publishers, 1946) and *Op Cite*. Keyes

only black and white. We are oftentimes confronted with paired words that are polarities such as either-or, all or none, right versus wrong, and good opposed to bad. One trouble with absolutes is that a single exception renders it invalid: the classic example being the assertion that "all swans are white." Not long thereafter, a black swan was discovered.

Lakoff[55] remarks that "[our] culture as a whole seems to have a problem with gray areas, preferring either-or to both-and or some-of-each."

Certain words should raise a red flag when they are on the tip of our tongue. Among these are "all," "always," "never," and "same." A wiser course is most likely when saying instead "many" or "most" for the "all;" "usually" for "always;" "seldom" for "never;" and "similar" rather than "same." This allows room for exceptions and other possibilities. One certainly should avoid making sweeping condemnations.

The person who habitually makes dogmatic assertions soon loses credibility. If he is in a position of authority and he demands and commands absolute compliance to orders, than there could be tragic results. Keyes[56] cites Ben Franklin in regard to his opinion of dogmatism. Franklin on his own as a young man came to the conclusion that his pronouncements containing the words "certainly" and "undoubtedly" did not endear him to his listeners. He discovered that these words usually ended discussions and he would find himself standing alone. He vowed to himself thenceforth to use such phrases as "I conceive," "I apprehend," "I imagine," and "it so appears." Thus, time proved him to be a wise man.

A third principle involving non-identity is that two things are never alike in *all* respects. Our generalizations carry us up to a point where things remain the same and treating them that way is efficient. Beyond that point they are different to the degree that it makes a difference.

---

[55] Lakoff, Robin Tolmach. The Language War (Berkeley: University of California Press, 2000). P. 37.

[56] *Op Cite.* Keyes. P. 152.

Generalization by its very nature is that some things are left out. Johnson[57] suggests that much of our confusion with language is because "...there are more things to be spoken of than there are words with which to speak of them." Group words (all collectives and abstract nouns) such as man, dog, house, California, tree, etc. leads us to think that "...we are talking about something definite and specific...."[58] A sign stating "beware of the dog" has varying significance if the dog is a pit bull rather than a Chihuahua. Similarly, the statement that "I love California weather" means one thing concerning San Diego and another concerning Yreka (in the northern mountainous region). Are we foolish enough to think that when someone tells us "I'll be back in a minute" that we will see him return in sixty seconds? If we are given directions that include the remark "it's a few miles beyond," are we expecting a precise two or three digits to roll over as we gaze upon our odometer?

The use of words often require further elaboration. We can get into trouble by treating them in an automatic, non-reflective way. We must remember that words are *just* labels and significant details may be omitted.

A fourth principle has to do with the dimension of time. Our words in a sense remain the same while reality changes. Keyes offers an enlightening anecdote[59] that illustrates the difference [I paraphrase freely in the following]. Mr. Johnson's wife experienced severe abdominal pain late at night. He telephoned the family doctor and reported her distress, adding "I'm certain that she has appendicitis." "No, no," responded the doctor, "it's nothing more than a little indigestion." He recommended a common anti-acid pill. The following day Mr. Johnson's wife was in excruciating pain. He called the doctor again The doctor irritatingly said "non-sense Mr. Johnson, I removed your wife's appendix two years ago. You know as

57 *Op Cite*. Johnson. P. 115.
58 *Op Cite*. Keyes, P. 93.
59 *Op Cite*. Keyes, P. 111-12.

well as I do that that couldn't be it." "That's true enough," responded Mr. Johnson, "but I have a new wife."

An example with much wider implications is raised by Lakoff having to do with the question who defines the self. Along with various cultural influences, she cites Freudian thinking concerning the determining factor that the unconscious mind plays in our memory. "If we can't trust our memories, there is no identity—no 'I'—we can claim with certainty." She should know and we should know that self¹ is not self². It should be no mystery that time changes and that we change with it. Our self-image (self-concept) is not fixed in concrete. Our perceptions of ourselves and our memories, whether absorbed directly from those around us or whether filtered by our own conscious minds, are subject to revision. We don't remember "everything" and we know that we forget a lot. The forgetting may be very selective. Our failing to have a sense of "I" is very remote (as might occur in dementia), but the "I" we do have is never static. Unfortunately, supporting Lakoff's larger point, the self-concept may be unduly influenced by our own inner irrational impulses and the social and political forces that surround us.

The high value our culture places on consistency is illustrated by the recent presidential election. Every effort possible was made to link political candidates with their past records. Opponents looked back ten to twenty years or more to paint others as "liberals," "conservatives," "being soft on crime," "favoring the tobacco lobby," etc. inconsistent with their current political stances. Unfortunately, the absurdity of this did not occur to many voters or media commentators. Why would one not change his point of view over a period of years *consistent* with a changing reality?

A fifth principle relates to the differences that location can make. The California weather example cited above applies. People tend to behave differently when with different people. Commonly, a group of men exclusive of women act in a way unlike how they would if females were present. In

---

⁶⁰ *Op Cite.* Lakoff, P. 36-8.

the company of children, adults alter their conversations. The man at work is different when he goes to the local bar for a drink with his social companions. The man who is chief executive of a major corporation is in a sense not the same man at home cooking steaks on his barbecue grill. The minister preaching in front of his congregation on a Sunday morning does not behave in the same manner as he would romping on the living room floor with his young children. A policeman directing vehicular traffic is not acting the same as when arresting a burglar. A psychotherapist may behave differently when shopping in a supermarket. Each of these examples illustrate the fact that we hold stereotypes about how people should behave under certain circumstances. Sometimes the role people exercise in different places are not stereotypes but are socially expected or legally binding. Such would be the case of occupation or profession. The bus driver and the physician have formal roles to follow.

Pragmatics takes into account the context surrounding a sentence that gives it broader meaning. Lakoff[61] defines pragmatics as "…the study of the relation between language forms and language function…." I interpret this to mean the purposiveness and effect of language. It would involve the intent of the message sent and the manner in which the listener or reader understands it. Unlike syntactics and semantics, pragmatics deals with feelings, motivations, and other social-psychological variables.

To borrow an example[62] of pragmatics: "*There's a car coming* is seen as, out of context, a statement that a car is coming. But in a particular context it might be a warning to a pedestrian not to step onto a road, an expression of hope that people invited to a dinner are at last arriving, and so on." The simple sentence alone cannot be understood by tying each word to its referent (their "truth conditions").

---

[61] *Op Cite*. Lakoff, P. 4.

[62] Matthews, Peter. The Concise Oxford Dictionary of Linguistics (New York: Oxford University Press, 1997). P. 290.

Lakoff applies linguistic theory (and pragmatics in particular) to the wider literary realm of narrative. It is in this form that most significant and meaningful communications take place. It is here where language can elevate us to the level of our full potential as authentic human beings or reduce us to the level of deceitfulness and hate (there are, of course, many *in betweens*)

Based on the semantic principles that we can't know everything nor can we know everything about anything, we must pay attention to the subjective component of language. We should be qualifying what we say more often than not with such phrases as "from my point of view," "as I see it," or even with the word "apparently."

Whatever we might utter, tells as much about ourselves as it conveys objective meaning. If I were to comment to a friend that the lady across the room was very attractive, I would be saying that I'm attracted to the woman as much or more than designating a creature who by some objective standards would be identified as beautiful. (Take note of the common saying that "beauty is in the eyes of the beholder"). As a male psychologist, I found myself on occasion describing a female client as being seductive in her interview with me. One day it occurred to me that I might be projecting and that it was I who was titillated in the presence of the woman.

If a person says that he enjoyed seeing the movies "Love Story" and "Apocalypse Now," it would mean at least that he is not totally put off by sentimentality and violence. Thoughts about liking something or otherwise evaluating from a feeling level is very self-revealing.

The self-reflexiveness of our language points to the strong determining effect our inner lives have on our perceptions, ideation, motivation, and utterances. As the old saying goes, we hear what we want to hear, believe what we want to believe. Our subjective world is a powerful force. Keyes[63] again offers a pithy phrase "mental one-sidedness."

---

[63] *Op Cite.* Keyes. Pp. 73-74.

We cultivate within our minds personal interests and our own points-of-view. These could lead to thoughts and behaviors others might label as biased. The formula of using a phrase like "as I see it" keeps open the possibility of entertaining other points of view. We can evaluate more realistically. We formulate for ourselves what meaning underlies our own language, that which we hold on to in memory and that which we express. We also give meaning to all that language others fling at us by way of the various kinds of media. Again, it is our well of personal interests and motivations that drive our interpretations.

Some "stupid" behavior can be the result of out-right ignorance. We may entertain mistaken ideas or we may simply have gaps in knowledge. The source of our ignorance may not always be our fault. We could, of course, begin with our formal educations from nursery school through the university. A lot of ignorance is institutionalized as content and by way of pedagogical methods. There is much we have to work on and try to remedy within ourselves and with existing schools. Another ever present danger concerning ignorance (incorrect meaning or gaps in knowledge) comes from others who wish to hoodwink us for their own reasons.

Lakoff[64] has brought to the forefront the problem of who is to define meaning. Her book's title, *The Language War*, does not exaggerate the case. There is a social, cultural, and political battle going on to capture our minds. Paranoid? No. 1984-ish? Yes, more or less.

Her thesis takes me back to the traditions of *formal debate*. Debate was (still is but less popularly) a structured contest in which the affirmative and negative sides of a proposition are advocated by opposing speakers. Typically a panel of judges designates a winner at the conclusion of the debate. Regardless of formal rules or fairness in arguing, many tricks are employed to win points for one's side. Similar tricks are used in ordinary discourse to achieve one's personal ends. Examples would be *name calling*

---

[64] *Op Cite.* Lakoff.

to denigrate one who would advocate a certain opposing view. Its opposite would be *name dropping*. One would seek an ally by calling on a recognized "authority," justifiably or not. Another is *populist appeal* to build strength on the back of "what most people think," "common sense," or "the majority opinion." It's said as though this makes it right. The debater or arguer might appeal to generally accepted prejudices. He might make false claims to support his argument such as "scientific evidence shows" when it doesn't. He might cite anonymous sources (can't be checked). Still another debating device is to deviate from the subject at hand, talking "beside the point." A favorite technique is to quote out of context (focus on the part not the whole). In this way, anyone could be construed as saying almost anything. Repetition of an assertion has a way of taking hold as being factual even when it is not. There are many more of these types of unfair tricks.

We cannot and should not seek comfort in formal logic. Arguments based upon the simple syllogism that if all A is B, and C is A, therefore C is B would be a logical conclusion. An example in words from Thouless[65] clarifies the validity: "All mammals are animals: All cats are mammals: Therefore, all cats are animals." The first two elements of the syllogism are referred to as propositions or premises. The logical conclusion is dependent upon both being factual. Unfortunately in many forms of discourse, one or both premises are not valid. If in the above example, we substitute the word "fish" for "animal" we must conclude that all cats are fish. Other syllogistic forms are subject to similar errors. Much depends on the accuracy of the premises.

Returning to Lakoff, we will find the vital importance of establishing meaning within ourselves and in society as a whole and who is in control of establishing that meaning.

---

[65] Thouless, Robert H. How to Think Straight (New York: Hart Publishing Company, Inc.,1932). P. 47.

The crux of Lakoff's conclusions rest upon the fact that our language is not static. It is changing continually. Existing words gain new meaning and new words come into being. There is the ever present need to revise our dictionaries. Changes are not simply the addition of new slang. The question is how are new words and phrases created? How do meanings change? Who is responsible for such changes? The answers are important because language determines our destiny. It defines who we are individually and collectively. It sets us on whatever course we and society take. "Language is," according to Lakoff[66], "the means by which we construct and analyze what we call reality."

In the past (and for most of us today), the accepted idea was that words and our language more broadly describe or represent the existing, present reality of things. It was as though meaning pre-existed the discovery of words. Not so. Our words are labels and how we link them together imposes meaning on our experience. That works pretty well in a static world. However, the world is far from fixed. Changes that come about through scientific investigation of the physical world call for a new vocabulary. For instance, we have the relatively new words of "cloning," "quarks," and "gigabytes." Not to mention the word "bug," now having the additional meaning of the source of a computer "virus." (Science sometimes gets smug about its language being more precise and tangible than social science and the humanities. Take a closer look and one finds that the structure and function of the atom and sub-atomic particles are identified by metaphor. No one has ever "seen" them). In the world of interpersonal relations and society's broader institutional structures, the dynamics of change are rapid and infinitely complex. Because of near instantaneous and constant media coverage through TV, radio, print, and the Internet, we may acquire new meanings from one moment to another.

Whoever controls the meaning of language wields great power. There are various elements within society competing for this power. There is a

---

[66] *Op Cite.* Lakoff. P. 20.

great division between what is loosely described as the power elite and the populace or the "establishment" and the "disenfranchised." The establishment are those who have had control in the past and who are holding on in desperation to retain it. The disenfranchised include a host of various groups that don't always share a common purpose. Included are women, Blacks, and a host of minorities such as Asian Americans, Hispanics, and Native Americans. The opposing forces are frequently described as "conservatives" and "liberals." They may further be characterized as Republicans versus Democrats. Groupings are made between "*us*" and "*them;*" between "*we*" and "*they.*" On top of it all is the media role as it relates to each and all of the other elements. The struggle is a *war.* It is so because it is a battle that affects the personal life of every participant.

Lakoff draws this picture in great and convincing detail. My focus is on some of the dynamics that enable the various forces to achieve their ends.

Oftentimes, we don't want to work our brains very hard. Critical thinking requires alertness and effort. We are not always up to it throughout a given day in our lives. So it is. But, we must recognize this reality and realize that at such times we can be duped by those determined to manipulate us for their own needs. We can be led by the nose, so-to-speak, to do stupid things.

One fact about language that demands critical analysis is that practically no proposition uttered or written has one, single interpretation. The intention of a speaker can never be known even when he tries to explain himself. The meaning we take from a message is partly our own meaning. Hopefully, we are in a position to have a dialogue with the message sender and ourselves. Thus, we might be able to take advantage of that wonderful mechanism of *feedback.* We can try and explain the meaning we obtained from the message to check it out. Mostly, our understandings are adequate for the demands of the situation—the mutual understanding is "good enough."

As previously mentioned, it is not as easy to deal with gray areas as it is to handle things in black and white terms. I remember as a child how comfortable it was to know that the good guys always wore white hats.

This was unambiguously reinforced in Saturday movie matinees week after week. Thinking in either-or extremes can lead to stereotyping and we seem to want to shape new events to support the stereotype. In the 2000 presidential campaign, Vice-president Al Gore was labeled (stereotyped) as stiff and unexpressive in feeling. Later, he was characterized as being aggressive and hostile. When he showed healthy assertiveness and enthusiasm, commentators interpreted it as being inappropriately aggressive.

The negatively connotative words purportedly describing Al Gore are similar to the technique of misusing metaphor. It might be said of someone's speaking voice that it is *shrill* or *whiney.* These are negative qualities one doesn't usually like hearing. To whine connotes weakness.

It is also more difficult to entertain new ideas as readily as to cling to the old familiar ones. We are comfortable having closure regarding our beliefs. The urge to maintain the *status quo* partly explains why conservatism has a much easier task holding its position than does liberalism, even when one discounts the latter word's negative associations.

Going against established authority or any controlling power is more difficult. The power elite possesses the tools for creating meaning. They usually have the money and "all the good jobs," CEO's and political leaders included. One must recognize this advantage and remain open to those having quiet and timid voices.

Unfortunately, we are suckers for the cute word or catchy phrase. The shocking expression or event gets our attention. Many have a heightened interest in the negative aspects pertaining to people, sometimes a prurient interest. The media sensing how such things will increase ratings latch on to the negatives or twist the story to make it sensational. We need to be aware of our vulnerabilities regarding these frailties to avoid having the media and others exploit us.

A first principle in the competitive battle to establish meaning is being the "firstest with the mostest." Getting your message out before your opponent can be crucial. You immediately go on the offensive. The

"Johnnie-come-lately" competitor is perceived as being defensive, reacting rather than being pro-active as the initiator had been. The public tends to latch onto and give credibility to what it hears first. It doesn't generally respond favorably to anyone in a defensive mode. The first to announce, to *leak,* or to publish determines the *twist* by which the meaning of language is filtered. The twist is quickly adopted because it seems to facilitate comprehension.

One can defend against having his thinking shaped in this fashion by becoming aware of it. Caution should be exercised concerning the party that is so quick to take the offensive. The sage advice not to jump to conclusions should be adhered to. Hold back and weigh as much of the evidence as is practical. One's opinion, the meaning one absorbs, and the choices made may be at stake.

The information media is becoming increasingly more potent in shaping meaning than ever before in our history. It is not only because of the immediacy, quantity, and diversity of sources. It is a qualitative change. As Lakoff[67] points out in her book, in the 50's and early 60's TV would carry a politician's speech in its entirety with little or no commentary before or after. Today, perhaps because of our lack of patience, we are offered snippets of the speech with a lengthy commentary.

We are sometimes told in advance what to expect in an upcoming event and certainly we are told afterwards what we had just heard (or what the commentator would like for us to have heard). Commentators or talk-show hosts and their interviewees offer predictions about the *significance* of something or other that is to soon transpire. Whether or not they are aware of it (they most likely are), the prediction may very well shape the meaning we give to the forthcoming action or communication event. I'm often amused by the sports commentaries that typically precede football games on TV. Admittedly, experienced professionals of the games can help us to be more intelligent viewers by informing us what to look for when a

---

[67] *Op Cite.* Lakoff.

game is underway. Even though they often contradict one another, no harm is done. Pre-event commentary is a different matter when it is a criminal trial, political matter, or significant social happening. These are serious and most often complex matters for us to make our own judgements. We can do without being propagandized in advance.

In this connection, we must be aware that questions often are an assertion giving the questioner's point-of-view. The response often doesn't matter. When hearing interviews or interrogations of various kinds, we need to keep in mind that the form of questions may be subtly conveying meaning.

We should question the question not only the questioner. Is the question too vague to answer? Is it designed to confuse the person to whom it is addressed? Is it formulated in such a way that the answer is verifiable? Certain words should be clues to problematic questions. Among these are "why?" A question in this form may call upon us to explain inner motivations. We may be unable or unwilling to do so. Another such word is "is" as in the question "what is your claim to success?" This is what may be called an *unlimited* question. We can't know when it is to end.

On our part, the failure to ask appropriate questions can lead to our downfall. We may not do so because we are too timid or we may not realize that our information is unclear, incomplete, or has been intentionally obscured. The way we formulate our question must be such that it requires a specific, verifiable answer. For example, if we are offered a bank loan at a reduced rate of interest, we should ask specifically what that rate is and how long it would remain in effect over the course of the loan. Granted, in putting such a loan into effect, we would have to sign documents amounting to a contract. You can be sure that the terms are likely to be in small print, easily overlooked.

Op Cite. Lakoff. Pp. 70-72.

We should beware of "common sense." One person's common sense may be another person's disaster. What makes sense common is that a large group (sometimes majority) of influential people claim to own the meaning of something or other. They usually can't support the fact that their meaning applies equally to everyone.

As previously mentioned with regard to semantics, we have some emotional reaction to all the words in our vocabulary. An association test to a list of words such as "mother," "chicken," "car," "Russian," etc. will yield a variety of feelings. Many of the responses will be held in common with others because of cultural conditioning. It is a strategy for those who wish to influence us to give special meaning to words and phrases that they ascribe to their opponents. This procedure is referred to as *rhetoric* and it has itself a negative meaning (Webster gives "undue use of exaggeration or display" as the most frequent definition). It is so often used by politicians that it should be regarded as a cliche. Among a number of rhetorical inventions listed by Lakoff, are *victimhood, liberal, radical, quota, special interests, family values, color-blind, fairness,* and *politically correct.* We need to know when we are being bombarded with these emotion laden words. They are being flung before our eyes and ears like arrows directed toward those who are regarded as undeserving, oppositional, or not one of *us.*

In public discourse, an antagonist might resort to shaming, demanding an apology, discrediting, and humiliating the protagonist. It's not fair even though there may seem to be logical grounds for doing so. Facts are required to establish meaning and sway opinion.

The use of humor can fall into the category of a "cheap shot," a cowardly act. Most comedians, political satirists, and cartoonists are not taken seriously. Their humor usually doesn't cross the line we deem to be within the realm of good taste. These are professionals doing what they get paid for—to make us laugh. On the other hand, there is the example of misapplied humor in the remarks Fuzzy Zeller made about Tiger Woods following the 1998 Master's Tournament. Zeller's words were thinly disguised racial slurs (even though Fuzzy vehemently denied such intent.

He apologized to Woods). The "just kidding" and "horse play" can be an excuse for displaying hatefulness. It must be seen for what it is and the hidden intent must be taken seriously.

A full accounting of the tricks of language would be sweeping and without end because new ones are being invented. The overriding point is that there is a battle over who controls the meaning of the language we employ. Meanings are of such great importance as to who we are and what will become of us that we want to determine our own meanings.

While speaking of language and meaning, a word needs to be said about *body language*. This is also referred to as non-verbal communication. We say a great deal, especially about how we feel, by our facial expressions, voice production and quality, mannerisms, and a variety of kinesthetic responses. Several years ago a famous Hollywood actress stated that interpersonal communication is seventy percent facial expression. As a great actress, she would seem to be a qualified authority on the matter.

An example of body language occurred in the 2000 presidential election campaign during the third debate between Al Gore and George Bush. Early in the broadcast, while Bush was responding to a question, Al Gore moved toward Bush to a position that was obvious to all as being very close. Gore appeared to stretch himself to his full height, stand at attention, and stare at Bush with a fixed and studied expression, with what I would call a half smile. Bush had a startled expression as he turned to look at Gore. My perception and interpretation may be biased when I say that Bush seemed to nearly slump in his posture and signal his feelings of being intimidated. I think many people perceived that act as an aggressive, intrusive move on Gore's part, designed to dominate Bush. That is how I felt about it and though liking Al Gore I did not admire that action.

The old saying that actions speak louder than words is typically understood to mean that we should follow through and do the things that we say we are going to do. That no doubt was the intended interpretation. I like to see a further meaning in the saying. It is that our non-verbal communication (actions) convey our genuine meaning. Our listener can *read* this body language, though most often at a sub-liminal level. The listener would like for the body-language meaning to be consistent with the content of the verbal communication. If not, he senses that the communication contains a "mixed message." He, like most of us, doesn't enjoy being confused. Body language is not a fiction. We need to pay attention to it.

Lack of Normal Skepticism

The most successful con artists know how to appeal to human greed. The idea of getting rich quick or just getting a good deal on a sale makes us vulnerable to the would-be swindler. We can understand how this happens because many of us have been sorely tempted in the past or have been victims ourselves. If we are naive, we are more likely to be victimized. It is commonplace for instinct to overcome our better judgement.

For many of us and all too often, instinct doesn't play a major role in our gullibility. It seems that we are too innocent, too simple, too trusting as a matter of course. We feel good about ourselves and think of ourselves as honest and straight forward in our dealings with other people. Thinking that others might not be the same way is disturbing to our peace of mind. It's contrary to the world view we have that people are basically "good."

It is here that we go wrong in our thinking. Being "good" or "bad" is just what either-or thinking is about. There is an infinitely broad span of grayness between the two. What one person deems bad another sees as "a little bit of naughtiness." What one interprets as a promise, another views as a "maybe." Between the good and the bad is the possibility of an array of "misunderstandings." Many of them having been construed in good faith. However, people are fallible. The world is imperfect. We must not lose sight of this fact. We think again of the Missourian, it is not too wrong when he asks "show me."

In advocating skepticism, I'm not disavowing trust. I speak of *reasonable* skepticism balanced against sensible faith. Since WWII when there was a burst of enthusiasm for psychology and the social sciences, the new adherents of these fields of endeavor were bent on proving that they were as good a "science" as were the physical sciences. Acceptance and prestige of a faculty appointment at a major university was often at stake. Consequently, we heard a lot about the application of the scientific method in our pursuit of knowledge. Some advocated this approach as the model for clear thinking in our everyday behavior. Although not altogether realistic, it's not a bad idea in principle. We start with a hunch or theory. We formulate a hypothesis to guide our inquiry. It is typically in the form of a prediction. The phrasing is such that it leads to an investigation that will yield supporting or refuting evidence. We make our observations in an objective and controlled manner to determine what the outcome is. We draw a conclusion from the findings and make them public so that others can verify it. It is at the point of having a hunch where healthy skepticism comes in. It allows for creativity. We challenge the generally accepted notions of what reality is and end up with new discoveries or a more secure hold on the truth about our world.

We must look to the special case of politics and consider the impact of electing potentially dysfunctional individuals to leadership positions. How can we avoid it? Behaviors that lead to voting for poorly functioning leaders include malaise, reliance on superficialities, lack of a discriminating attitude, selfishness and greed, and blind loyalty to political ideologies and parties.

Malaise can arise from the mistaken attitude that "one vote [the one you have the privilege of casting] won't make any difference." You might say "what's the difference, my vote will just cancel out my wife's vote anyway." Inactivity can come from the belief that it's not important anyway who's president. "One man can do the job as well as the other" or contrariwise "one party is as bad as the other."

As an argument against this, consider how the Cuban missile crises might have turned out if Richard Nixon were the president rather than Kennedy. Nixon's strong anti-communist stance, his frequent threat while in office "to use the bomb," and his machismo attitude all would work against the required patience and diplomacy. Kennedy had to stand alone practically against all his chief military advisers to avoid going to war. His delay in ordering a military strike against Cuba and Russian freighters was said by nearly all those being consulted as evidence of cowardice. Imagine what a spur to action this would have been for Nixon.

Malaise can come paradoxically from the "I'm too busy" syndrome. Snyder[68] cites a number of state and federal elections that were decided by one vote in our political history.

We make mistakes by giving importance to superficialities. Examples are physical characteristics like personal attractiveness, gender, race, and religious affiliation.

Do we know that we should pay attention and carefully evaluate what we see, hear, and read? Will Roger's famous quote that "All I know is what I read in the papers" was said in jest. Newspapers in his day were even more blatantly biased than they are now. But the same still applies, "we must not take the bait, hook, line, and sinker." We must investigate, at least in our minds, the sources of our information. We must not jump to conclusions. Don't allow one person's prejudice to shape one in yourself.

Selfishness and greed can lead to the wrong decisions. Special interest groups in political campaigns illustrate this. The 2000 election may be the clearest example of single-minded greed than of any election in our history. Here are a few of them: tax relief, pro-choice/pro-life, gun lobby, religion in schools, public funding of private schools, environmental concerns, tobacco companies, drug industry, oil producers, and so on. Are we to allow one or two of these favored positions to rule our overall judgment about what is best for ourselves and our country?

---

[68] Snyder, George E. Don't Be a Spin Sucker (Lincoln, Nebraska: Writer's Club Press, 2000). P. 91.

Ideologies and political organizations often rely on non-cognitive processes to acquire and maintain a following. There is a range of pressure to conform from the subtle "you are one of us" to the overt threat of expulsion or *elimination* "if you don't go along with us." Individuation is often thought of as the enemy of the group. "Don't think for yourself, think the way we do." Identifying with a set of beliefs or belonging to a group is not wrong, of course. What is wrong is to allow oneself to become totally submerged in the group, essentially relinquishing one's autonomy.

Impaired Self-concept

Before answering the question as to how the self-concept affects one's actions either positively or negatively, we need to explore the meaning and implications of the term itself. Most of us have a commonsense under-standing of the notion that goes somewhat like the definition offered by Webster[69]. It is as follows: "the idea or mental image one has of oneself and one's strengths, weaknesses, status, etc.; self-image." The field of psychia-try and some psychologists would regard the idea of self-concept as too vague. That it is important is evidenced by the fact that Webster's diction-ary has 949 definitions of "self" words (mostly hyphenated nouns and adjectives: the number does not include syntactical variations). I offer a definition that takes into account some implications of personality theory. It is that the self-concept is how one has *chosen* to define selfhood based on one's own apprehension of strengths, weaknesses, status, etc.; and based on conscious evaluations of the inner content and workings of one's mind. Body concept is incorporated as derived from one's own perceptual expe-rience. (Selfhood is the state of being an individual person, having indi-viduality and personality).

---

[69] Webster's New Universal Unabridged Dictionary (New York: Barnes & Noble Books, 1996).

An important corollary to the above definition has to do with the phrase "one has chosen." Psychological theory varies greatly as to the source of the self-concept. A common point of view in the past is that the self-concept is derived from our infant and childhood experiences. Additionally, it is believed that once established it becomes determined invariably. More recently, the thinking has been otherwise. It is now more often said that our current cognitive functions impact the nature of our self-concept. It is more flexible than previously thought. The corollary I offer takes an intermediate position. It relates to the notion of *locus of evaluation*. We commonly make judgements based on inner personality determinants or other (outer) personal or social pressures. The ability to make decisions based on internal criteria (inner determinants) has to do with two things. One is a distillation of core meanings from life experiences. It starts not long after birth and should continue throughout life. The process revolves around personal needs and how they mesh with physical and social reality. Evaluation occurs, driven by feelings and cognition. There is differentiating and generalizing concerning our encounters with these realities. Two is the courage to act on these inner resources, giving them at least equal emphasis to the demands of the external world. Maturation occurs within the typical personality, moving from greater dependence on forces outside oneself to greater reliance on what some have referred to as the core of being. Jourard[70] phrases it as "real-self-being." These expressions capture the meaning of the self-concept or self-image.

A person's self-concept as a directing force plays a significant role in personal satisfaction, in his relationship with others, and in the world that he encounters. The self refers to one who has complete individuality. The saying *one's own self* encapsulates the meaning. Self is to be understood in the existential sense: *I am*. It is to be understood in the sense that it is *I who initiates action*. It is to be understood in terms of the *I having*

---

[70] Jourard, Sidney M. The Transparent Self (New York, D. Van Norstrand Company, Inc., 1964).

awareness of I. Each plays a part in the concept of self. Each affects one's being in the world.

Of the 949 dictionary self words, a few stand out in illustrating things about the self-concept. A number of them relate to self-appraisal. Among them are: self-esteem, self-respect, self-acceptance, self-satisfaction, self-liking, and self-love. A number refer to appraisal by oneself or by others. Included are: self-confidence, self-directed, self-determined, self-aware-ness, self-disclosing, self-consistent, selflessness, and self-centered. Three other frequently encountered self phrases are genuine self, true self, and authentic self. The last are essentially synonymous. On the negative side we have the unintegrated and the undifferentiated self. Persons burdened with these negatives have a fuzzy, confused core of being. All of these self words and phrases give a feel for how one's self-image is central to person-hood. The self-concept will determine our place in the world: what impact we have on the present and future.

The Prevalence of Deception

When it comes to speaking the truth, we are sometimes in a situation where faced with the choice of telling the proverbial "white lie." We may be asked a question that seems to demand it for a smooth, congenial rela-tionship. When your date for the evening asks whether or not you like her new gown, you are not likely to say "frankly my dear, I don't give a damn." You also are unlikely to say that you think it's unbecoming to her. A more likely response is that "you look ravishing in it!" This is a somewhat trivial situation to illustrate the reality that the truth is relative to time and place. A not so trivial example is the predicament of the American POW's in Korea. Telling lies about the U.S. role in the war kept many of them from being executed by the enemy. In such circumstances, should they have been punished for lying?

How many times have we heard the plea "let's be totally honest." It might be a prelude to hearing the naked truth spoken by someone we may or may not consider an adversary. We would probably brace ourselves to hear something shocking. On the other hand, it might be an appeal to us to tell what's deep within our heart without censoring our opinions with ordinary tactfulness. We would probably find it a challenging undertaking. One might believe it to be wise and justifiable to say "I'd rather keep my opinions to myself." A justification would be that such a case is not speaking to the fact but would be offering a subjective opinion. You have the right to the privacy of your own mind, perhaps our greatest freedom.

Nevertheless, lying is ugly. It also can create problems as alluded to in the famous words of Sir Walter Scott: "O, what a tangled web we weave, When first we practice to deceive (*Marmion*, Canto VI, stanza 17)." One may lie to save one's own skin. One may lie to manipulate others. He may lie habitually where there is no personal advantage or gain. The direct consequences of a lie may be to do another harm. There is little or no defense against such a lie.

We swear-in witnesses in a court of law conventionally by having them place their hand on the Bible and uttering "so help me God." It is assumed that there is a deterrent in such a procedure. First, traditionally a good many people felt that God would strike them dead if they were to lie following such an oath. Second, the swearing established a point in time when failure to tell the truth, if discovered, could result in the penalty of perjury. Lying is likely to be seen as stupid in such circumstances.

The behavior of former President William Jefferson Clinton as previously noted, was in dispute as to whether he committed perjury under oath or whether he simply exercised his right not to disclose potentially damaging information. His interpretations of what specific words meant

---

71 Fierman, Louis B. Effective Psychotherapy: the Contribution of Hellmuth Kaiser (New York: Collier-Macmillan Limited, London, 1965).

were a pivotal point. Again, it is not always clear as to what lying is (like the "is, is"). Clever or stupid?

There is another form of lying. It issues as much from self-deception as from dissembling with others. The psychoanalyst, Hellmuth Kaiser,[71] developed a theory of the universal neurotic symptom. He called it "duplicity." Webster defines this word in much the way Kaiser used it. Duplicity is "deceitfulness in speech or conduct; speaking or acting in two different ways concerning the same matter with intent to deceive; double-dealing." This is lying that oftentimes has a slight twist. It comes close to if not being the exact play on words employed by Clinton. There are two sides to the meaning. You conceal one side and allow the other to stand as the intended meaning. It is declared neurotic by Kaiser because it becomes habitual (is at times unconscious); it covers up one's own unacceptable thoughts and feelings about oneself; and it is self-destructive. The words the neurotic utters are to conceal his genuine self from others (and perhaps from himself) and to manipulate others to fulfill his own ends. It is indeed ugly, neurotic, and stupid.

Core of Sinfulness—Self Centeredness

Sin. How objectionable that word has become in modern discourse. The reasons why have been documented thoroughly by the famous psychiatrist, Dr. Karl Menninger[72]. Much of what in the distant past had been called sin, was labeled crime from the middle ages on. Then under the influence of Freud in the early 1900's and the evolution of modern psychiatry and psychology, sin became illness. Society's progression from the religious to the secular made people reluctant about moralizing. People seemed to take to heart the admonition "judge not that ye may be judged (Math. 7:1)." Along with scientific relativism, came less judgmentalism.

---

[72] Menninger, Karl. *Whatever Became of Sin?* (New York: Hawthorn Books, Inc., 1973).

There remained a degree of discomfort about people not being responsible for their acts. One wondered what had become of freewill. If sin had disappeared, where was our exercise of free will? There also was the commonsense view that some acts of man are just plain wrong. There are "thy shalt nots" that have nothing to do with a criminal or sick mind. Most of us had to contend with our consciences regarding some matters. It wasn't always the persistent voice of the imperious super-ego. At times, the conscience seemed to rest on some solid moral grounds.

The crux of the moral issue is expressed in the following comment by Menninger[73]: "Sin is not against the rules, but against people—and it is the 'against-ness' or aggression in the intent or motivation that constitutes the designation sin." There is still meat in the ancient "seven deadly sins" consisting of envy, anger, pride, sloth, avarice, gluttony, and lust. A refined definition of each in current English makes it obvious that they are alive and well. As most of us encounter them, we feel their unpleasantness, offensiveness, and anti-social qualities. To elaborate on three examples: *pride* (though having a positive aspect) underlies arrogance and self-adoration. Likewise, *lust* is the expression of sexual drive in a way that tends to destroy the personality of those participating. Sexual infidelity is a violation of trust and integrity. It is a destroyer of relationships. The show of *anger* can range from rudeness to physical violence. It invariably involves an effort to exert power over others.

The most accepted, single religious definition of sin is alienation from God. The secular one is self-absorption. It is most apparent in the narcissistic character disorder. The term is derived from the Greek myth concerning the youth named Narcissus. There are several versions of the story but they all have in common that the lad was extremely handsome and one day he bent over a stream to take a drink and saw the reflection of his own face. He discovered how handsome his face was and immediately fell in love with it. Before and after he had no love for anyone. He stayed by

---

73 *Op Cite.* Menninger. P. 134.

the stream and subsequently died. A flower grew at that place and it was given his name.

Narcissism is thought to stem from a failure beginning in infancy to separate self from those who are nurturing. The valuing of self is dependent upon a constant "feeding" from others. This results in a vague and tenuous sense of selfhood and absence of genuine self-esteem. This is where the mirroring aspect becomes more than a figure of speech. The individual's self-image and self-respect is derived from the attention others provide him.

Paul Tillich[74] gives us some insight into the narcissist with his understanding of the term self-love. This expression often has a positive connotation as with the Biblical reference "you shall love your neighbor as yourself (Gal. 5:14). Tillich believed that self-love is a metaphor and it should be understood as self-affirmation. The narcissist doesn't affirm himself. He obtains his affirmation from others.

I not only focus upon the narcissist because he exemplifies the sin of self-absorption. I give it special mention because it is a personality type that seems to be endemic in today's society. Martin Buber[75] offers us an interesting distinction about people. He sees them relating in either an "I-It"or an "I-Thou" mode. In the former, an individual views other persons as things. In the latter, an individual relates to others as persons. The "I-It" reaction to other beings is in my terms "thinging"them. It is what the narcissist does. A simple illustration is the feeling and actions one displays towards the super-market cashier. In that formal but brief encounter, is the cashier a thing performing a function or is the cashier a flesh and blood person having a great deal in common with oneself?

The narcissist finds other people important only to the degree that they flatter him or perform a useful service for him. When others are not

[74] Tillich, Paul. Love, Power, and Justice (New York: Oxford University Press, 1954).
[75] Buber, Martin [Trans. by Kaufmann, Walter] I and Thou (New York: Charles Scribner's Sons, 1970).

important or not useful, they simply don't intrude upon the narcissist's consciousness. It is as though the others don't exist. A case in point is when a group of friends are engaged in watching a particular program on TV. The narcissist in the crowd pushes the control button to another channel without saying a word to anybody and wants to keep it there.

Empathy is a function beyond the experience and comprehension of the narcissist. He cannot divine the needs of others. He doesn't understand it when others try to explain their needs. He volunteers little in the way of doing for others. If he does so, it is for personal gain or show. They are usually blatant manipulators. They can *play* a role if it is demanded of them. There is no substance to it.

The narcissist likes to treat themselves to the better things in life. They like to puff themselves up and adorn themselves with expensive accouterments. Their lives bring destruction on those who come within their sphere of influence. They manifest bad judgment, stupid behavior, and the worst of the sin of self-absorption.

The horrors of WWII resulting from totalitarianism, sparked interest in the state of mind that would produce the Hitler's and Mussolini's of the world. Adorno[76] began research in 1943 on anti-Semitism being aware of the persecution of Jews in Nazi Germany. Not long after, Allport[77] published *The Nature of Prejudice*, thoroughly reviewing the broad aspects of prejudicial thinking. Efforts were made by Adorno and others to devise personality measures that would reveal tendencies toward authoritarianism and intolerance.

In 1960, Milton Rokeach[78] published a book outlining his research and methods of testing the concept of the open and closed mind. We often use

---

[76] Adorno, T. W. et al. The Authoritarian Personality (New York: Harper Brothers, 1950).

[77] Allport, Gordon. The Nature of Prejudice (New York: Doubleday & Company, Inc., 1954).

[78] Rokeach, Milton. The Open and Closed Mind (New York: Basic Books, Inc. 1960).

the expression of "open mindedness" in describing someone in a complimentary way. It's reverse, closed mindedness, is used in a pejorative sense. These are diametrically opposite mind sets that lead to differing world views. These traits are not simply dichotomous. They fluctuate within a person depending upon varying situations. Generally, the closed minded person assumes his cognitive mind set under conditions of personal threat. The threat may be against his sense of security, safety, or self-esteem. The threat may be perceived as ever present or transitory. A threat to one person may be a simple annoyance to another. However, the traits may be more or less fixed comparing various individuals. Some may be rigid in their closed mindedness while others show considerable capacity for adjusting to change.

Two factors come into play regarding closed mindedness. One has to do with an individual's vulnerability to perceived threat and the extent to which he responds with fear and anxiety. The second relates to his manner of coping. There is an element of irrationality, perceptual inaccuracies, and increased reactivity. Rokeach portrays the closed minded person as having "…a tightly woven network of cognitive defenses against anxiety. Such psychoanalytical defense mechanisms as repression, rationalization, denial, projection, reaction formation, and over-identification [described subsequently] may all be seen to have their representation in the [closed minded] belief-disbelief system…."

The closed minded is more inclined to disregard potentially contradictory evidence in an argument. He seeks only those opinions which are affirmatory of his own viewpoint. He tends to be more single-minded and over-determined in his thinking—that is to say dogmatic. He is more dependent upon blind authority. The closed minded person's perception of time is skewed in the direction of remote future events that are difficult to evaluate. The relevance of the past, present, and near future escapes him. There is a strong need for structure in his world view. He has low tolerance of ambiguity and he has difficulty entertaining cognitive dissonance. Thus, it is often compelling for him to seek answers consistent with his own security needs.

The closed minded are likely to be regarded as being opinionated, bigoted, intolerant, and on the radical right politically. The extreme manifestation of closed mindedness is found in cults, militia groups, skin heads, etc. The character trait even in its milder forms can lead to considerable grief for the individual and society. Those who function at a higher intellectual level are capable of greater mischief.

Threats to an individual's sense of safety, security, or sense of personal integrity are not infrequent in society. The sources of threat may be variations of external circumstances They also can emanate from within. Threats may come from natural events such as earthquakes and drought. They may come from a variety of life forms such as viruses, sharks, mad bull elephants, and human beings. We generally think of fear as a reaction to real, external dangers, such as the charging elephant or the burglar wielding a gun.

The word "anxiety" is commonly reserved for feelings associated with anticipated fearful events or other mental processes that for some reason or other are scary to us. Most often fearful events occur suddenly and are just as suddenly over. Not so with anxieties. They generally nag us for a very long time. There is usually a self perception of unreasonableness to the experience of anxiety. We commonly can't identify any specific reason for the anxious feelings. In fact, the entire notion of psychodynamics as understood by psychoanalysts and personality theorists, is that repression keeps us from knowing what it is that is troubling us. Typically, such things as childhood conflicts that were unresolved at the time of occurrence remain with us in our adult unconscious minds. This process is suggested as being the source of our anxieties. Well they may be and they can cause havoc in one's life.

There is another postulated source of anxiety that is likely to play a major role in how a person conducts his life. This is what is called *existential* anxiety. Man, the only creature having conscious awareness of his own impending death, has anxiety because of this knowledge. Man's existence is a matter of "being-thrown-into-this-world."[79] The individual man did not willingly obtain life for himself and he cannot willingly ward off the inevitability of his dying. This reality is difficult if not impossible to avoid through denial. Existential anxiety remains in the shadows if not in the forefront of one's consciousness. A characteristic but debilitating response to such anxiety is to seek security in conformity. The man attempts to escape his knowledge of his own finitude and its accompanying anxiety by seeking comfort in the mundane. Anxiety that is not faced realistically can direct one along paths fraught with danger.

In this chapter I described a wide range of behaviors and conditions of man that can lead even smart (highly intelligent) people to say and do things that would be regarded according to varying criteria as stupid. It is not an exhaustive list. I've omitted plenty of details for want of space and there is room for the undiscovered. The many predicaments in which an individual may find himself are not all hopeless.

---

[79] Breisach, Ernst. Introduction to Modern Existentialism (New York: Grove Press, Inc. 1962). P. 86.

CHAPTER VI

What of Additional Factors That May Underlie Stupidity?

Those Behaviors Where Freewill is in Doubt

There are certain classes of behaviors that may be devoid of conscious, rational choice. We might have to say in a number of instances that some behavior—stupid as it seems—isn't the result of "stupidity." When we are making value judgements about people, we need to keep in mind that for some reason or other they may not be responsible. It is not only kind and humane to do so but it also has practical value. A brief illustration would be interpreting the behavior of a reckless driver. Such a person may be in a diabetic coma.

In some cases, we can be very certain of our conclusions. This happens when we evaluate something tangible, something we can subject to laboratory or other objective testing. The diabetic driver could offer conclusive proof as to why he was driving his car erratically. Other behaviors can be a little mystifying and elusive when trying to determine responsible judgement. We can find this problem on occasions in a court of law when judge or jury must determine criminal responsibility. They might have to decide

128

whether a defendant is: "not responsible because of insanity," "not capable of assisting in his own defense," "acted upon an irresistible impulse," or "was unable to exercise reasonable control over his actions."

Impulsiveness. The Webster dictionary offers the definition of "actuated or swayed by emotional or *involuntary* impulses [*Italics* mine]." The psychiatric dictionary[80] gives a more refined definition but one not too far off that offered by Webster. The more technical one goes as follows: "In general psychiatry, impulsive usually applies to swift action without forethought or conscious judgement. In most cases this word refers to the impulses for action, which are accomplished unexpectedly, without real reflection, or without the assent of the whole personality."

Most of us can say that we have observed such behavior in people. We are likely to say that we see it as characteristic of some of our friends, acquaintances, or our enemies. We might liken them to lighthearted, spontaneous, interesting people. However, their unpredictability might be annoying and their actions might take on the character of riskiness. The latter might reflect that portion of the psychiatric definition which states acting without "conscious judgement."

Impulsiveness in itself is a descriptive word. It does not tell us what drives it or the why of it. In some examples, those who manifest impulsive behavior do so because of some neurological defect. The person may have at some time in his life suffered a head injury resulting in damage to the brain. There may have been a congenital defect or an infectious disease of some kind resulting in brain damage. Much progress has been made in the medical and psychological evaluation of these conditions.

Some children have been diagnosed as having an impulse disorder that seems due to a malfunction of the brain. Encephalography has verified this problem. Such children have been described as having a low tolerance

---

[80] Hinsie, Leland E. and Campbell, Robert Jean. Psychiatric Dictionary: Fourth Edition (New York: Oxford University Press, 1970). P. 387.

for frustration and a tendency to explosive outbursts when things don't go their way.

There are some impulsive behavioral patterns that have not been so readily detectable by laboratory testing. Among them are hyperactive disorder. This problem, unfortunately, is rather prevalent among children (from 5 to 7 percent). It appears that there may be an increasing number of them emerging with this disorder. An underlying physical cause is likely, substantiated, in part, by the fact of their often having a favorable response to medications.

Sigmund Freud has attributed impulsive acting out as emanating from the unconscious or what he has described as the "imperious Id." His idea seems to gain support when considering other classes of impulsive behavior. Among them are kleptomania, pyromania, exhibitionism, voyeurism, sadism, masochism, and pedophilia. If people act in these ways, they might find themselves in court on criminal charges. At such a time, they may plead "not criminally responsible because of an inability to control their impulses." Such may be the courts ruling and an effort would be made to have the individual enter psychotherapy. Therapy is often difficult because there is a pleasurable component in the symptom and the individual doesn't experience distress regarding his self-image.

Compulsions. Our psychiatric dictionary describes these problems as "repetitive, stereotyped, and often trivial motor action…." They occur despite the individual's wanting them not to happen. Efforts to refrain from the actions result in distressing anxiety. Completion of the acts bring temporary relief. Compulsions are overt behaviors. Obsessions are similar in character but they remain a part of one's thought processes.

A common behavior which most of us engaged in as children was stepping over the cracks in the sidewalk. For those of us that found it a passing thing, it was like a game. Where it persisted to the point of personal annoyance, it became a compulsion. Doodling can be a compulsion as would be graffiti. The scribbling of obscenities on bathroom walls clearly shows a sexual dynamic. Another fairly common compulsion among adults, perhaps more than children, is repetitive hand washing. It can become such a commanding urge that a person might do it fifty or more times a day. Needless to say, one's life would seem to be out of control. A person's skin can suffer mightily. Persistent bleeding is common. The seemingly stupid behavior is in fact neurotic.

Habituation. I employ this term in a very general sense. I use it to mean that we form habits of thought and action. They are dependent upon memory but distinguished from memory in that they have a repetitive characteristic in response to external stimuli. They oftentimes have the feeling of being an automatic response. They may come forth without apparent attention or thinking. I distinguish habituation from addiction because the latter has the added feature of physiological dependence.

About 1900 the Russian I. A. Pavlov introduced the concept of "conditioned response." Since then, we have become aware of complex human reactions that seem as mindless as the knee jerk. Some common examples of habituation that nearly all of us are aware of have to do with motor acts. Once gaining the skill of riding a bicycle or driving a car, we don't think about the mechanics of doing. Regarding driving a very familiar (and usually boring) route, we sometimes become aware of driving for several miles without being conscious of where we had just been.

Habituation can serve us well or it can lead us to disaster. It is fine most of the time regarding the motor acts described above. It is useful with respect to our routinely brushing our teeth without much complaint. Typing on the computer key board is a highly prized habit.

When we respond in a situation in a habitual manner and that situation is not routine, we may be in for trouble. For example, driving that road with our minds on our upcoming vacation won't cut muster if the bridge has been washed out a few moments before our reaching it. Addressing one's girlfriend by an old flame's name won't win us a warm response. Jumping off a diving board into a pool just drained of its water doesn't bode well for your physical well being. Being the usual good guy and going along with the crowd without question can have a sorry outcome for you if the crowd is on a stupid or dangerous mission. We can run a great risk by relying on habit when we should hold back and apply a reasoned approach. One must know and respect one's habits and not shut down completely an awareness of the tasks that may be at hand at a given time.

We are responsible for the creation, maintenance, and application of our habits. We also are responsible for the memories we fashion and cherish. They help to define who we are.

Relinquishing Command of Ourselves. There are all too many times and situations in which people seem to put their cognitive abilities into the deep freezer. They function in a mindless way. Strangely, this will happen with the average Joe on the street, the brain surgeon, and the nuclear physicist. The phenomena is no respecter of age, intelligence, or social status. Typically, an individual will function intelligently in most areas of his life or at least in his vocational field, but suspend his judgement in some other area such as in the political or religious arena. For the outside observer, this can be mysterious and exceedingly frustrating. We often long to understand it and we would like to bring it to an end. I find three broad categories in which people find themselves mindless.

1. There are those who suspend their judgment in favor of others, such as their chosen group. The group might consist of a parcel of friends, gang, fraternity, church congregation, or political party. Such a response is encouraged by a culturally determined pressure to go along with the majority. Don't be a party-pooper is what we hear. This is consistent with the so often quoted phrase "peer pressure." It is perhaps the major determinant for teenagers who start smoking or engage in unprotected sex.

In the same class are those who abdicate their responsibility to an authority figure of some kind. The authority may well be a spouse, a boss, a politician, or the main guy in a church hierarchy

We are familiar with the idea of a charismatic leader. The word "charisma" was unknown to me until I was studying sociology as an undergraduate in college. I don't think it was a frequently used word during my youth because I don't remember it ever being applied to explain the likes of Adolf Hitler. Perhaps this was because, as I learn from the

Oxford Dictionary of English Etymology[81], it was originally a Greek word meaning "free gift of God's grace." Thus in the beginning, it was a theological word. I learn more from Webster's dictionary. It states that charisma is a special spiritual power or personal quality that gives an individual influence or authority over large numbers of people. Furthermore, there are "special offices, functions, positions, etc. which confers or are thought to confer on the person holding it an unusual ability for leadership, worthiness, or veneration...." Now we have evidence of a broadened definition that would apply to both heros and villains.

The charismatic phenomena is a serious business. This is clear from the examples of Hitler, Charles Manson, James Jones, and David Koresh. We should ask, how does this happen? Is it a gift of God granted to particular individuals? Is it something in a person's genes and formative period that gives rise to it? Is it some combination of personality, office or position, and receptive followers?

I believe the answer is in all of the above. In my early professional experience, I had a boss who fit the description of a charismatic leader. He had his good points as well as bad. He exuded control and command so extraordinary that it was mysterious. Thus, there was an element that seemed to be divine. I gave this man respect and loyalty as a boss. I was enthusiastically committed to fulfilling his every wish so long as they were not detrimental to my own best interests or contrary to regulations. I liked the man and, in fact, I loved him as I would a father. I was under his "spell" only up to a point. That point was defined by the previously stated phrase "so long as they were not detrimental to my own best interests or contrary to regulations." There is a self-protective element within my personality for good or bad that prevents me from being swallowed up by an ideology or person. If I feel I'm about to be overwhelmed, I pull back almost fearfully and tell myself I have to reflect upon this. I do it at a gut

[81] Onions, C. T. [Ed.] The Oxford Dictionary of English Etymology (New York: Oxford Press, 1966).

level and can't thus claim any special strength of character. I sometimes wonder if I were an ordinary citizen in Nazi Germany would I have succumbed to the prevailing doctrine.

I'm aware of two German theologians who repudiated Hitler (many didn't). One was Paul Tillich and the other Diedrich Bonhoffer. The latter was executed by the Nazis toward the very end of WWII. These men of principle were able to stick to their basic beliefs that transcended the human condition. Charisma held no sway over them.

There perhaps should be an additional commandment that "thou shalt not divest yourself of your responsibility to choose." Those who give up their decision making bring to mind the humorous song from the late fifties or early sixties titled "The Devil Made Me Do It." It also reflects rationalizations in the following vein: "it's my parents' fault." and "I grew up in a poor environment."

When looking at both private and public organizations, we run into a special kind of situation. Here we have both hierarchical organizational structures (thus delegation of authority and responsibility) and group decision making. These open the door for the individual to excuse himself for the choices made. Harry S. Truman is noted for the saying that "the buck stops here." This is the way it should be in a hierarchical system. Many a fired football coach is well aware of this concept. He cannot credibly blame his assistants, players, or "tough schedule."

Organizations commonly make decisions by committee. The ground rules for deciding may be by majority opinion, by consensus, or in some other manner. Whatever, individuals cannot in good conscience relinquish their responsibility.

2. Among the three classes of relinquishers are those who are best described as *oblivion seekers*. Webster again helps out by including in his definition the following: oblivion is "the state of forgetting or being mentally withdrawn." Those wanting to achieve that level of unconsciousness must be driven to escape some very painful inner voices or the awareness of terribly distressing reality. It is here that we find those who are addicted

to something or other. Substance abusers include alcoholics, drug addicts, sniffers, smokers, etc. These entail a physical dependence upon the substances that are abused. It usually means a build up of tolerance so that it requires more and more of whatever it is to achieve the desired effect. Abrupt disuse of the substance results in withdrawal symptoms that might end in death.

The term addiction also has been given to shop lifters, gamblers, and sexual offenders. There is some laboratory evidence that they experience some alteration in their brain chemistry while engaged in their peculiar activity. Thus, there is some parallel to the physical dependence of the substance abuser.

Generally the law doesn't favor them with an excuse when their addictions lead them to criminal acts.

Why do people seek oblivion? Why do they become addicted? Previously mentioned was the need to escape some inner or outer demons. In the case of substance abuse, it is a matter of getting started. Social pressures of various sorts play a significant role. Parents might model an addictive life style. Peers may be a strong influence. Advertising could increase the probability of substance abuse by imprinting the product name on the mind's of youth, by desensitizing viewers or listeners to the dangers, and by romanticizing its use. Once started, the same factors reinforce continued use. The increased tolerance factor may enter in and it takes more and more to achieve the "right feel." Addiction can thus take hold. The need to escape reality becomes pronounced because there is a new reality of the addictive life style.

Without doubt certain people are physiologically prone to substance abuse. There is likely to be a genetic factor that plays a role. As with nearly all behaviors, genetics alone would not be the sole determining factor.

3. Among the list of relinquishers is a very special group. They are those victimized by the mind control technique known as "brainwashing." During the Korean War between June 25, 1950 and July 27, 1953, the Communist Chinese perfected this method on our POW.'s. The modern day impetus for this approach probably came from Joseph Stalin when he

shifted his strategy from warfare to the winning of people's minds for communism. He had a scientific model for doing so in the work of the Russian physiologist Ivan Pavlov. No doubt precursors would be in the likes of Genghis Khan and Tamerlaine who centuries before effectively neutralized and dominated vast numbers of people. Subsequently in 1950, some brilliant and enterprising Chinese army officer devised the brainwashing strategy for our Korean POW's.

The Chinese brainwashing approach fell into two broad phases. Within the first six months of the war when the vast majority of our P.O.W.'s were captured, prisoners were subjected to extreme hardship. A good number of them had to endure long death marches that were even harsher than the Bataan Death March of WWII. Men were beaten, executed, and starved. They were poorly clothed for the extreme winter weather. They were commonly placed in isolation in small cubicles where they had to live in their own excrement. The names of prisoners had not been revealed so men suffered realizing that their families did not know whether they were dead or alive. They also felt that the Chinese would have no compunction about killing them since there was no record of them being in confinement. They had witnessed the murders and death through abuse of many fellow prisoners, and they were thus aware of the tenuousness of their own survival.

On the twenty-second of December 1950 a new phase began when a special indoctrination camp was established in a new prison camp designated as Camp 10 in Kanggye. Two hundred and fifty selected men were exposed to three months of intensive "education." From the extreme conditions of deprivation, they were suddenly treated in a favorable manner. They were issued new clothing consisting of blue shirts, trousers, and caps consistent with the attire of Chinese students. They were given haircuts and shaves. Their food was improved in quality and quantity, supplemented by candy treats and cigarettes.

These two hundred and fifty men were divided into two companies of 125 men each. They were further subdivided into squads of ten men each. Each squad had its own hut and the men were kept apart from those in other squads when not under supervision. Training went on for a minimum of ten hours a day every day of the week. It began with a mass indoctrination speech each morning lasting for three to four hours. The men then returned to their squads and discussed the morning speech. Each man had to prepare a written summation of the speech and discussion. They then had to listen to readings of communist literature read aloud by one of their fellow prisoners.

In addition to the indoctrination of communist ideology, a good deal of time was devoted to the criticism of capitalism and the American government. The communists hoped to obtain the prisoners' cooperation to propagandize the American public and the rest of the world against continuance of the war. They wished to label the U.S. as "the new Nazis."

After three months, Camp 10 was disbanded and the "graduates" were spread out over the other camps to set a model for the indoctrination program being universally implemented.

Strategies that led to the successful indoctrination program included the following. Immediately upon capture, officers and non-commissioned officers were stripped of all authority. Everyone had to function on an equal level under threat of death. This resulted in confusion and lack of structure. It played a significant role in the men's feelings of total isolation from fellow prisoners.

Chinese interrogators would question and harangue a prisoner hour after hour and day after day.

Men were duped into signing confessions on the grounds that they were advocating a world peace movement. A soldier was quoted as saying: "[It's] not a crime to fight for peace and talk about peace...."[82] They often signed blank papers.

They were rewarded for cooperation by candy and cigarettes. Access to tobacco was a major motivator.

---

[82] Lech, Raymond B. Broken Soldiers (Chicago: University of Illinois Press, 2000), P. 102.

In spite of positive rewards, the threat of death by execution for recalcitrance was ever present.

Men were encouraged to inform on others. They felt that anything they said got back to the enemy. "One sergeant recalled that he would not have trusted anyone, even his own brother."[83]

They had "criticism meetings" wherein they informed on one another about trivial, daily-life issues to ideological matters.

Rumors were rampant. Conscious fabrication of rumors was commonplace among the men. Often, the Chinese planted their own rumors to spread dissension.

Chinese interrogators and educators often spoke American English fluently. They were masters of American idiom and slang. This occurred because many were graduates of the University of California and the University of Chicago.

One reason for the Chinese success was the fact that following WWII the U.S. military was recruiting men having very marginal educational achievements and intellectual abilities. They were nearly totally ignorant of American history, civics, and our economic system. They also commonly came from disadvantaged homes that had not shared in the fruits of our democratic and capitalistic system. However, many well educated and privileged service men, including many officers, did succumb to the brainwashing. Most notable was the marine corps' Col. Frank Schwable who was among the most decorated of heros from WWII. He was Chief of Staff of the First Marine Air Wing at the time of capture. He had been subjected to the most extreme forms of mental torture. "For five months he was held incommunicado, left to languish in his own filth within an unheated 3 X 7-foot hole, constantly subjected to hammer-like reiterations of interrogators." Col. Schwable described his long experience of

---

[83] *Ibid*. P. 155.

[84] Leckie, Robert. Conflict: The History of the Korean War (New York: Putnam, 1962).

[85] *Op Cite*. Lech. P. 176.

"mental torture" as worse than physical torture would have been. Following his release, a psychiatrist who interviewed him stated that he was "without a will."

The Chinese characterized those who cooperated as "progressives" and those who did not as "reactionaries." There were a number who fell in between by maintaining a low profile. Of 6000 American prisoners, fifteen percent collaborated. Only five percent actively resisted. Of the 6000 total, 2,370 died while prisoners. Of the latter total, 1,036 were murdered.

Among the collaborators were about "75 U. S. soldiers [who] had agreed to spy for the Communists or act as their agents after repatriation to America, and 23 more did not want to return home at all."[86]

Fourteen repatriated POW's were subjected to court martial upon returning home. The entire judicial proceedings against those few were subject to considerable controversy then and now retrospectively. There are strong reasons to believe that their rights were flagrantly abused. The U. S. military drastically revised its code of conduct for prisoners of war. Previously, a captured service-man had to give only his name, rank, and service number. He had been ordered not to cooperate with the enemy and to seek escape if at all possible. Less than a month following the truce, a lengthy new Code of Conduct was promulgated. A part of section VI of the code reads as follows: "I will never forget that I am an American fighting man, *responsible* for my actions, and dedicated to the principles which made my country free [*Italics mine*]."

A number of psychiatrists (a hundred and fifty had been involved in doing evaluations) and other close observers believed that this POW experience was a major contributor for our ability to understand and cope with the phenomena of brainwashing. A civilian attorney for one defendant is quoted as saying: "…I do now realize that Claude Batchelor's tragic plight imports a great social problem and a stern ethical warning."

---

86 *Op Cite.* Leckie.
87 *Op Cite.* Lech. P. 241.

Another glaring example of brain washing resulted from the Symbionese Liberation Army's kidnapping of Patricia Hearst, heiress and granddaughter of the famous William Randolph Hearst. She was abducted on February 7, 1974 from her college dormitory. She was nineteen years old. She was held as a prisoner for eighteen months. She was subjected to sensory deprivation for extended periods, repeatedly threatened with death, raped, and flooded with indoctrination. She was coerced to issue a public statement that she was joining their cause and soon thereafter was compelled to assist them in holding up a bank. Patricia was rescued (apprehended as a fugitive) late in 1975. She went to trial for bank robbery and in spite of being defended by the famous defense attorney, F. Lee Bailey, she was convicted and sentenced to seven years in prison. Her sentence was commuted by President Jimmy Carter after her serving two years. In January 2001, President Bill Clinton pardoned Patricia after Jimmy Carter's persistent efforts to see that justice would finally be done.

Without doubt Patricia Hearst's prosecution and conviction was a terrible miscarriage of justice. Her kidnapping at the hands of violent, ruthless political activists and her subsequent treatment by them closely followed the brain washing techniques perfected by the Chinese communists. At the time of her experience, these techniques were summarized as inducing the three D's on the captor, debility, dependency, and dread.

It is worth noting that some of these brainwashing tactics are now frequently used in cults, militia groups, and terrorist organizations. Specific tactics in this genre are sometimes applied in more benign groups such as school classrooms, church congregations, college fraternities and sororities, and business and government organizations. At issue is the curtailment of free choice and personal responsibility.

Subliminal Messages and Hypnosis. Psychological research on humans had established the phenomena of subliminal perception. The word "liminal" is derived from Latin meaning threshold. There is a small range of intensity of stimuli—whether auditory or visual—where a person "registers" experiencing the sensation but is unaware of exposure to the stimulus. In other words, there is a threshold where consciousness does not play a part. Some twenty years ago movie theater managers introduced feature film previews that briefly flashed images of the word "popcorn." People generally didn't "see" the word because it appeared for only a fraction of a second. Nevertheless, many more people were induced to leave their seats to buy popcorn than would have otherwise. Subsequently, the government outlawed the practice.

In the presidential election campaign of 2000, someone associated with the Republican party did a similar thing in a TV commercial by flashing an uncomplimentary word about Vice President Gore. It created a sensation but the Republicans denied any responsibility. The outrage clearly signaled the general belief that the practice was unethical. What does this mean? It simply shows that there is one more way in which human behavior is affected without conscious control.

This raises a question about advertizing because one way or another a promoter will try to induce you to buy his product. Though not directly employing the device of subliminal perception, there are plenty of very peripheral cues directed toward changing your attitude and feeling level. All this to make you more receptive to a sales pitch whether you are conscious of it or not.

There are new TV advertizing strategies that employ a potent hypnotic technique. The sound and images of the commercial immediately introduce confusion or confusion coupled with distraction. The psychological effect of this is to arouse attention and cause the individual to restructure his mind set. At the time of this restructuring, the individual has increased receptivity to new ideas. If you think about your TV viewing experiences, you might recall that much of the commercials' content seem totally unrelated to the products' name or the product itself. You feel that you have to fill in the blanks.

Clearly, what pertains to advertizing will also apply to propaganda. We associate that word as a method of psychological warfare. However, we might get it every day from anyone intent upon changing our minds toward their desired ends.

There is no way that such mind control strategies can be outlawed. It goes against free speech as provided in the first amendment of the Constitution. If permitted, such a law would be impossible to enforce. Being aware that techniques exist that are designed to influence us one way or another without our complete understanding and consent, may help to defeat the effort.

Still another form of influence that we might voluntarily subject ourselves to is that of hypnosis. It can be a powerful tool in changing attitudes, behavior, and state of mind. It has a number of helpful dental, psychiatric, and medical applications.

However, there are several dangerous myths regarding the hypnotic technique. One is the belief that a person can't be hypnotized against his will. It's not so. A person can be duped into a situation where a hypnotic procedure is applied. Even so, a person can proclaim that he can't be hypnotized and he will be. Another myth is that a person cannot be made to do something under hypnosis that he wouldn't otherwise do. It's not so. Again, the person can be duped one way or another to do something because of a changed perception of reality. Also, repeated hypnotic trances over a long period under an unethical person can steal away the persons sense of autonomy, essentially yielding his will to that of the hypnotist. A few years ago, such a case was adjudicated in a criminal court absolving the hypnotized person of a crime.

Those Behaviors Resulting from Mental Impairment

There are a great many types of mental illness. The American Psychiatric Association periodically publishes a manual that lists and describes them. In a way, the manual serves the purpose of identifying the universe of behaviors we label as mentally ill or deviant. Generally, diagnoses are descriptive. They are based on various symptoms (observable or measurable signs) that fit together into what is referred to as a syndrome. Thus, a particular illness is identified.

These syndromes as a whole cover a broad range in terms of the descriptive aspects of human behavior. They differ as to apparent causes and methods of treatment. They differ as to prevalence. They differ regarding age of onset They differ as to duration of symptoms and periodicity. They differ as to how seriously they affect one's life adjustment. They differ with respect to personal insight and subjective suffering. They differ as to prognosis.

Mental illnesses, in general, occur proportionately among various races, ethnic groups, and nationalities. Historically, in all probability most of them have been with us since the dawn of man.

Commonly, there are people suffering from one form of mental illness or another who are in our midst and we aren't aware of it. This may be so even with the so called major mental disorders. One reason for this is that some illnesses are episodic. Another reason is that modern treatment methods are very effective. Usually the best approach with the major illnesses are a combination of what is called milieu therapy, psychotherapy, and chemotherapy. As a result many people have been deinstitutionalized and are adequately treated on an outpatient basis. (Exceptions are those who are unwilling to engage in treatment programs. This has resulted in swelling the ranks of the homeless street people as are the now proverbial "bag ladies"). The point is that we may see "odd" behaviors among those in our circle of acquaintances or among those we have casual contact with. Some behaviors may appear to be the result of stupidity when they are not.

Impaired Sensorium and Brain Damage. The role of the central nervous system (CNS) which is made up of the brain, and spinal cord is of great importance in defining a human being. Of course, the body is an integrated whole but it is the CNS which provides this integration. The brain itself is the seat of what we regard as "mind." It is what defines us as humans beings and distinguishes us as individuals. It is the functioning mind that gives rise to consciousness and leads to self-awareness. From this self-awareness, there evolves the idea of "self," our being distinct from other beings. We gain, in time, a sense of autonomy and freewill. Much of this is a maturational process. Unfortunately, at any place in our growth and development from the pre-natal state to an advanced age we can suffer damage from all sorts of internal and external forces. When such happens, our human functions and potentials may be impaired.

1. The sensorium is the sensory apparatus of the body. It is what keeps us in touch with the world, the world beneath and beyond our skin. It consists of the five senses we are certain of possessing: sight, hearing, feeling, smelling, and tasting. Feeling aids us in determining the pressure of touching, awareness of temperatures, vibrations against our skin, and pain. A combination of senses, especially the workings within our ears, gives rise to what is called kinesiology. This we commonly know as balance and movement. Along with vision, it lets us know where and how we are situated in space. Imagine its importance regarding our perception of reality. The importance is readily apparent to anyone who has been in an earthquake.

Permanent damage to a part of our sensorium results in the loss of some freedom of choice. Physical impairments of this nature frequently are not readily apparent to an outside observer. Consequently, we might observe stupid actions that are not a result of "stupidity."

2. Damage to the brain itself can occur as indicated above at various stages in an individual's development. The source of damage can include genetic variation, problems at conception, difficult birth, invasion by some infectious agent, environmental poisoning, radiation, and head trauma. These many potential hazards make it easier to understand that there probably are few individuals alive today who can claim that they don't have some degree of impairment to their CNS. Fortunately, much of this would be mild and fortunately, too, the brain is remarkable in its ability to compensate.

Brain injury itself can affect the peripheral nervous system because of its coordinating function. By this means, we can observe kinesthetic and various other motor disturbances. Speech can be distorted in one way or another because the physical mechanisms giving rise to speech production are damaged. Such would be the case regarding tongue movement, swallowing, and breathing patterns.

Brain injury is likely to affect what we know as cognitive abilities. This can relate to the speech example because the neural pathways within the brain associated with language and speech production might be disturbed. Other cognitive abilities, such as what we commonly refer to as thinking, may be affected. Further still, we are likely to observe many peculiarities in the emotional life of the individual. Such may manifest itself in interference with mood states (ranging from depression to elation) and with overt behavior such as rage reactions. Again, we may see people acting in ways to which we are unaccustomed. It does not necessarily indicate "stupidity."

Major Mental Disorders. Aside from brain damage as we commonly know it (which often is major in its effects), there are a group of serious illnesses that have in the past been described as "functional" in nature. The "functional" label was applied because there had been no demonstrable relationship to structural damage in the CNS. In more recent years, this view has been changing because of correlations between these illnesses and such things as encephalography, genetics, and response to chemotherapy. Many of the illnesses have a long history, having been described with considerable accuracy by medical practitioners in the last half of the nineteenth century and in the early years of the twentieth. Interestingly, we can find references to similar behaviors by physicians and philosophers during the Golden Age of Greece.

The prevalence of these illnesses are such that some of their names are well known to us. Such is so for schizophrenia, manic-depression, and paranoia.

1. In the early 1900's, a psychiatrist named Eugen Bleuler introduced the term "schizophrenia" to replace that of *dementia praecox.* The latter term literally meant precocious dementia—essentially a psychosis of young people. Bleuler believed correctly that the chief characteristic of the illness was a split with reality (not a split personality as many think). Sufferers had difficulty determining what was real from the not real. Common symptoms included hallucinations of various sorts and delusions. Also, as science developed methods of peering into the mind so to speak, such as evaluating artistic productions of patients, it became clear that the subjective world of the schizophrenic was filled with perceptual distortions. As time went on, it also became clear that schizophrenia was not a unitary disease (a parallel can be drawn with cancer). There are many forms of it, each having different characteristic behavioral manifestations. However, the split with reality links them still, as do a few other features.

Schizophrenia can occur in childhood. If it is going to occur, it usually does by the late teens and early twenties (not precluding occasional later onset). It can vary in its intensity and it plainly follows a different course from one person to another. Some people respond exceptionally well to medications (about two/thirds) while the remainder struggle. Contrary to a general belief, those suffering from schizophrenia are no more prone to criminal acts than the public at large.

It is quite possible for us to encounter a person having the diagnosis of schizophrenia during our normal routine. We are not likely to notice anything out of the ordinary. If we do see something that appears to be the result of stupidity, it may not be.

2. A manic-depressive illness generally differs from schizophrenia by primarily impacting mood, by being periodic (even cyclical) in its appearance, and by individuals essentially returning to their normal selves during periods of remission. There is very strong evidence of it being a genetically caused illness. Some individuals are only depressed, some only manic, and some both in a cyclical pattern. Initial onset is usually before the age of fifty. It usually responds well with medication, but

chemotherapy compliance is sometimes poor with those prone to hypomania (a milder level of elation and hyperactivity) and manic episodes. There is often an accompanying euphoria experienced as pleasurable, and patients enjoy the feeling to the extent that they don't want to take medications that will bring them off the high. Impulsive actions and poor judgment are characteristic of a manic phase. Commonly, people engage in reckless spending sprees and carefree, promiscuous sexual adventures.

3. Paranoia is both a symptom and an illness. As a symptom, it may be summarily described as baseless suspiciousness and hypersensitivity. Some individuals express these traits from very early in life and the traits persist throughout their lives. In many interpersonal situations it leads to a distortion of reality. It is often said of them that they use very poor social judgment. Now, we all are sometimes overly suspicious and too sensitive with respect to our feelings. But with most of us it is a *sometimes* thing. For us, it is not persistent and certainly it is not a pervasive personal trait. The question arises with respect to those showing paranoia whether or not they are acting in a stupid fashion. The answer is "yes" but not because of stupidity. They are manifesting a personality disorder.

Unfortunately, this condition is all too prevalent in society. It does vary in degree of severity from one individual to another. It can form the bases of judgmentalism and prejudice. In its more extreme forms, it can lead to patterns of borderline behaviors such as affiliating with hate groups and extremist militia factions. Because of its importance, I cannot refrain from quoting at length from the American Psychiatric Association's manual of mental disorders.

> [For the paranoid personality] Almost invariably there is a general expectation of being exploited or harmed by others in some way. Frequently a person with this disorder will question, without justification, the loyalty or trustworthiness of friends or associates.

Often the person is pathologically jealous, questioning without justification the fidelity of his or her spouse or sexual partner.

[They are] typically hypervigilant and take precautions against any perceived threat. [They have] transient ideas of reference, e.g., that others are taking special notice of them, or saying vulgar things about them. [They are] usually argumentative and exaggerate difficulties, "making mountains out of molehills." They often find it difficult to relax, usually appear tense, and have a tendency to counterattack when they perceive any threat. Though they are critical of others, and often litigious, they have great difficulty accepting criticism themselves. [They appear to others] as keen observers who are energetic, ambitious, and capable, but more often they are viewed as hostile, stubborn, and defensive. They tend to be rigid and unwilling to compromise, and may generate uneasiness and fear in others....They display an excessive need to be self-sufficient, to the point of egocentricity and exaggerated self-importance.

Extend the suspiciousness a little further and we may have the psychotic illness of paranoia. Gradually, one may develop systematized delusional states while preserving one's normal intellectual integrity. However, the individual's emotional responses and behaviors are consistent with the content of their delusional ideas. Common examples are the belief that the FBI is trailing and watching them. Their telephone is tapped. Even more bizarrely, they have the notion that the FBI implanted listening devises somewhere under their skin. They make such claims as fact without the least distortion in their thinking processes. It's the premise that's wrong; not their logic. We may call these behaviors unreasonable or stupid, but not because of "stupidity."

Other Definable Psychiatric Problems. We have knowledge of other mental problems such as psychoneuroses and disorders of personality, character, and behavior. Some are arguably capable of impairing one's ability to make responsible choices. Often it is not easy to discern whether or not someone is so afflicted. But regardless of that, when it comes to criminal responsibility such problems don't get an individual totally off the hook. A sympathetic judge or jury may go easy on them because of the extent of their personal suffering.

An Array of Different Types of Thinking, Feeling, and Behaving. Superstition is a phenomenon that we are all familiar with whether we engage in its use or not. The broadest definition is any blindly accepted belief or notion. It is not based on reason or factual knowledge. Most superstitious beliefs are aimed at warding off some sort of potential evil but there are many having to do with obtaining good fortune. An example of the former is to not walk across the path of a black cat: of the latter is the athlete who won't change socks from one winning event to another ("it might break my string of luck"). We acquire many of these ideas from folktale. We also acquire them by contingency. When two events accidentally coincide, we tend to attribute a causal relationship to them. This is like Pavlovian conditioning. The bell rings and the dog salivates. The driver of an automobile always makes a point of avoiding the shortest route to his house. He does so because on an earlier occasion when driving that particular road he experienced serious chest pains. He was in a near panic believing he was having a heart attack. Associating that episode with driving that particular route, he changed from what would have been his preferred way to go home. Such would be a habit that is difficult to extinguish because there can be no negating evidence. By not driving that way again, he will not have *any* new experience either to confirm or deny the assumed causality.

When Freud wrote about the psychopathology of everyday life, he had in mind principally how the unconscious mental processes affected how our memory malfunctioned. He cites endless examples of forgetting names, mistakes in word order, misapplication of house keys, etc. He generalizes "that the forgotten or distorted material becomes connected through some associative path with *an unconscious stream of thought* which gives rise to the influence that comes to light as forgetting [*Italics* added]."[89] Examples he gives are very innocuous but they might ordinarily be thought of as stupid. Among many instances cited about the use of keys, he writes of a Dr. Jones who reported that while conducting some important and interesting work at home, he was called to go to the office. When arriving there, he mistakenly used his house key in the office door lock. The two keys he says are vastly different in appearance and he carries them in different pockets. He reflects upon the cause of the stupid error and decides that it reflects his wish (at that time not within his consciousness) to be at home rather than at the office.

There are many other mental gyrations associated with unconscious processes that Freud failed to go into when writing about everyday events. Over the years these have been identified as "defense mechanisms" but more recently the preferred term is "adjustment mechanisms." The word "defense" was employed to identify them because it was believed that the conscious mind defends itself against the undesirable workings of the unconscious. Substituting the word "adjustment" is a way of broadening our understanding so as to embrace the notion that mental mechanisms are adaptive. They help us deal with emotional needs and stresses. Adjustment mechanisms operate outside of conscious recognition to insure protection of our need for security and self-esteem. Although they are a product of habit, they work as instinctively as self-preservation responses would in the face of physical danger.

All of them share the characteristic of easing our anxiety as well as the characteristic of distorting our perception of either inner or outer reality. The various mechanisms can be scaled roughly along a continuum from minimal to optimal degrees of distortion. Thus it is that habits of the mind lead to the expression of mindless or stupid ideas and actions. Lets

---

[89] Brill, A. A. [Ed.] The Basic Writings of Sigmund Freud. (New York: Random House, Inc., 1938).

begin at the low end of the scale where there is the least distortion of reality but the greatest prevalence of usage.

1. **Rationalization** is false reasoning to explain our behavior. It occurs so commonly and the word is used so often that it is frequently thought to mean rational thinking.

It is a cover-up for the real or primary motives driving our conduct. Since we would find those motives to be unjust or embarrassing, we hide them behind false explanations to preserve our self-esteem. It is not lying since it is an automatic, unconscious process. Most if not all behavior has multiple causes. Usually when we are driven to act by instinctual, selfish motives, they are the most potent. They are the "real," true us. But they are either suppressed or repressed in favor of self-justifying, weaker, socially acceptable motives.

Rationalizations have a negative effect because they are self-deceptions. They serve as an untrustworthy guide for our behavior. Subsequent conclusions adhered to on the basis of earlier rationalizations may form the basis of future decisions, ones therefore, that would rest on shaky ground.

2. **Identification** is one way we establish who we are. In this manner it is a perfectly normal function. We latch on to the characteristics of other people or representations and adopt them as our own. Much of our sexual identity, for instance, stems from identifying with our parents. As we mature, we turn to other role models to help establish our sense of self.

We also identify with groups and ideologies. Loyalty and attachment to a particular sports team can be very intense. "My this" and "my that" reflects identification. We may prize belonging to a political party. Problems enter in when our identifications are uncritical allegiances to a role model, group, or ideology.

A positive form of identification is the time limited experience of empathy. It is the capacity to put oneself into another's shoes. It is getting their feel without losing one's own objectivity. The ability to empathize is a sign of maturity.

3. **Introjection** is mostly a normal childhood phenomena. It is the automatic taking in to the undifferentiated self the values of good-bad, accepting-rejecting uncritically from the valuing source. It is a primitive form of identification and the opposite of another mechanism to be discussed later—projection.

4. **Incorporation** is the unexamined reintroduction of a formerly rejected object of identification. Since the previous rejection was likely based on a negative emotion, the negative feelings are operable but remain alien to the sense of self.

An example would be going along the same path of a parent, a path you disliked and rejected. And one you continue to reject in the parent and in yourself. A mother might be distraught about spanking her child for she belatedly recognizes her own mother acting through her.

5. **Compensation** is the effort to enhance self-esteem or hide deficiencies whether real or imagined. A classic example is the short person who feels inferior because of it. To save himself from this persistent, unpleasant feeling, he compensates by developing an aggressive and dominating manner. He thus believes that he is a "big fellow," one tough to contend with because of his strength of character.

When this mechanism goes to the extreme, we speak of over-compensation. One could, for example, develop delusions of grandeur. Possibly this was a factor in the developing psyche of Adolph Hitler.

6. **Substitution** occurs when one is strongly committed to a particular goal but for some reason believes he cannot obtain it. Continued struggling for it or total surrender of it is not forthcoming. Accepting a less desirable but somewhat related goal is the choice.

Someone aspiring to become a dentist gives up and accepts in its place a career as a dental hygienist. This might appear to be an admirable adaptation. It might well be if further struggle toward the original goal would have been, in fact, a futile enterprise. Also, the substitute choice would make sense if it were the best of possible alternatives. However, we do often hear the plaintive, regretful cries "if I had only tried harder" or "if only I had done something totally different."

7. **Restitution** is a way of relieving one's guilt by trying to make up for what was thought to be a previous wrongful act or acts. It is a pattern with some wife abusers to be extraordinarily attentive and generous with their wives between violent episodes.

There have been those who spend their lives trying to be outstandingly "good" and generous as restitution for real or imagined wrong doing as children. Conceivably, it might be a motivation for saintliness in an overly scrupulous religious person.

8. **Reaction formation** is employed as are most of the mental mechanisms to keep from awareness unacceptable desires, impulses, or strivings. It does so uniquely by affirming or acting out the opposite of that which is unacceptable to the conscious mind.

Look beneath the over-determined assertions or behavioral patterns for the reverse responses and you find the particular fearful, forbidding urges of the unconscious.

The overt perfectionist covers a felt, inward turmoil of imperfections that challenges his confidence about remaining in control. The obsequious person is likely to be loaded with buried anger. The aggressive person is insecure. The submissive is aggressive. The amiable is hostile.

Reaction formations can explain the origin of many prejudices, biases, and intolerances.

You might find a snake handler who abhors snakes or a mountain climber who fears falling.

9. **Displacement** is the transfer of feeling from one object, situation, or person to another. This is necessitated because the original target for the expressed feeling was taboo—forbidden by conscience or some other strictures. An example regarding persons would be hateful feelings toward the unacceptable parent target being placed on someone resembling the parent in looks, behavior, or position, such as a future boss. Fear of one's sexual urges may be vested in a rape phobia.

10. **Suppression** as opposed to repression is a *conscious* process of casting from awareness undesirable or anxiety provoking thoughts or feelings. It is related to avoidance and purposeful forgetfulness. It is like putting a lid on a jar of problems and placing the jar on the shelf, perhaps to be taken down later, perhaps not.

It has its positive side as expressed in the sayings "don't cross the stream until you get to it," "why worry unnecessarily," or "put it out of your mind until you have to deal with it." However, not taking the jar off the shelf may be a maladaptive way of handling reality.

11. **Compartmentalizing** is placing related ideas or feelings in separate little boxes of the mind so that they cannot connect with each other. The process has been referred to as maintaining "logic-tight" and "affective-tight" compartments. It is undergirded by the unconscious mental mechanism of rationalization which says in effect "this doesn't fit here, it fits there, and that fits somewhere else."

Some of these compartments can represent reality and others fantasy. They go on their merry way simultaneously without contradiction. There is no possibility of self-correction. It is a sorry state of affairs and it is all too common among people otherwise regarded as normal. It explains how a molecular scientist, for example, can believe in the a literal reading of the Bible.

12. **Avoidance** consists of an uncontrollable reluctance to encounter situations, objects, or activities that represent unconscious sexual or aggressive impulses or the circumstances where those drives might be subject to punishment. This mechanism is central to the neurotic illness known as *phobia*. An inordinate fear of ascending heights may reflect aggressive urges directed toward the self.

13. **Symbolization** is when one idea or object is used to represent another idea or object which thus becomes symbolic of the first. The symbol carries the emotion and meaning of the original object but it does so entirely outside awareness. It is a convenient way to let potent, restive unconscious urges to find the light of day—that is to enter awareness in disguise.

The man who wore bright red socks to his therapy session believed he was being fashionable or daring. His therapist saw it a different way. The therapist believed his client was expressing anger towards him.

The listener who repeats the phrase with an edge of impatience "I understand, I understand" is saying in effect "I wish you would shut up." Likewise the repeated utterance "really!" is saying "I don't believe you."

14. **Fantasy** (phantasy) is thinking that turns away from reality to seek gratification of one's unconscious and unacceptable wishes and desires. Unable to achieve direct fulfillment of urges, the individual turns to illusion and imagery.

The sexually repressed man may perceive himself as a dandy. He may engage in flirtatious gestures towards others but would flee from any overt response of acceptance. Literature's best example of an elaborate fantasy is found in *Don Quixote*.

Fantasy has its positive side as does day dreaming. It approaches vivid imaginings that might foretell how particular circumstances in the future might be. Both it and day dreaming may siphon off the energy of strong instinctual urges thus aborting possible self-destructive, overt behaviors.

15. **Intellectualization** is the process of diverting emotionally charged material into the sphere of the intellect. Personal affective content is not addressed because it is elevated to an abstract, theoretical level. The underlying human experience becomes a philosophical or theological conundrum. To hear this from another, one might feel like saying in the common vernacular "come on man, get with it!"

16. **Isolation** as a defense mechanism doesn't relate to being alone. Rather it refers to a condition where the mind isolates one part of consciousness from another. One aspect of awareness may be regarded as unsavory and through isolation it is made to stand alone or off by itself from all other meaningful connections. An example would be to have an intense jealousy towards someone but rather than experiencing the feelings one fantasies the person suffering a great humiliation. The painful

jealous feelings don't reach awareness and there is no feeling of guilt about the person's misfortune.

17. **Undoing** consists of an action that is opposite what the ego is compelled to reject. It is best understood by example. White[90] relates an incident where a teenager regarded another boy, a known masturbator, as evil. Although the teenager vowed to avoid the evil one, he found it difficult to do so. As he passed by the boy, he turned and, without conscious intent, spit in his direction. He thereby "cleansed" himself and expressed rejection of the other boy immediately after the danger of contact. The act of spitting was the undoing, an expression of disgust rather than the acceptance he could not permit himself.

18. **Ideas of reference** are not uncommon among teenagers and other persons who might have transitory social fears. This is the uncomfortable experience when you feel that everyone in the room is staring at you critically for some suspected inadequacy. It could be a part of the proverbial "wall flower" character.

Ideas of reference can become pathological by degree if you believe the others wish you harm. In serious forms, the others' normal conversation is interpreted as accusatory or denigrating. In other words, there is a move from a simple anxiety to delusion. It is a projection of self-criticism on to others.

19. **Dissociation** can be a very dramatic defense mechanism. It is at the bottom of the commonly known syndromes of dual and multiple personalities. It is the condition in which a broad aspect of one's psychic life is separated from one or more other segments of one's awareness. The separated portion of the personality is beyond the control of normal consciousness. In multiple personalities one character is unaware of the existence of another.

In addition, dissociation accounts for somnambulism, otherwise known as sleep walking. Dissociation accounts for fugue states in which

---

[90] White, Robert W. The Abnormal Personality: A Textbook (New York: The Ronald Press Company, 1956). P. 283.

individuals' consciousness are altered and they follow aimless, wandering activities. These may last only for brief moments but can go of for days. They are frequently followed by amnesia.

20. **Projection** plays a part in other defense mechanisms and it may be seen in individuals we would deem as normal. However, it can be very serious because of frequency, duration of use, and near total disregard of reality. It can become bizarre and psychotic in nature.

It serves as a defense against anxiety by casting unacceptable attitudes, traits, and motives within oneself onto others. A common example is the person who constantly ridicules others for the very traits that he himself should claim. Another example is the individual who maintains that someone in particular hates him and wants to do him harm. The fact is that the suspicious one himself harbors intense feelings of dislike towards the other. He experiences a desire to hurt the other.

Projection blinds oneself to one's own dynamics and distorts the perception of the outer world. It fuels cynicism, pessimism, prejudice, and intolerance.

21. **Denial** is the unconscious process of rejecting aspects of the self or events relating to the self that are unacceptable. (One must understand that the word "denial" as used to identify this mental mechanism, is not the same word we are familiar with in ordinary discourse. When one exclaims that he *denies* something to be true, he is making a conscious assertion. The denial mechanism is employed automatically without conscious direction as is true with nearly all of the mental mechanisms). Denial is making some portion of reality non-existent. Those successfully employing this mechanism usually have a weak ego. The Willie Loman from the play "Death of a Salesman" is a good example. He is an obvious failure but maintains the facade of being successful. Others are the amputee who believes himself whole or the parent who continues to believe that her deceased child is still living.

22. **Repression** is the granddaddy of all mental mechanisms. Unlike denial, it deals solely with banishing from consciousness unacceptable

desires, strivings, ideas, and tendencies toward forbidden actions. All other mental mechanisms may exist to cover those occasions when repression fails. The derivative instinct and the idea and the feeling associated with it may be repressed *in toto* or each separately. The energy associated with the repressed content is not destroyed. On the contrary, that energy is constantly seeking expression in some way or another. The result, because consciousness does not come into play, are various quirks of the personality. Unflattering traits, prejudiced belief systems, neurosis, and psychosis may be the result.

All these ways in which the mind functions are directed toward the distortion of either or both our inner or outer experiences. The ability to optimize adjustment to every changing reality is thus abrogated. Hidden motives can lead us astray. Automatic, unthinking responses and repressions of various sorts interfere with conscious and flexible adaptations. We must learn to recognize, understand, and control our defensive or adjustment mechanisms in order to be realistic and efficient in perceiving, choosing, and controlling ourselves in this complex world.

Hormonal Factors

Hormones are substances that play an essential role in the functions of a living organism. They are closely bound atoms serving as message carriers. There are various kinds of hormones that serve different functions such as controlling growth, metabolism, food utilization, response to emergencies, and sexual determination and function. In the male, the latter are otherwise known as androgens that have their origin in the testes. One that receives major attention is testosterone.

Testosterone is commonly thought of as the male hormone and estrogen as the female hormone. This is an accurate labeling but potentially misleading because males and females carry both hormones. On the average, males have ten times the concentration of testosterone as do females (however females are more reactive to small amounts). There is wide variability in testosterone levels within both sexes at any given age. Generally, the amount of testosterone is very small in the embryo and after birth. It increases to a peak in the late teenage and young adult years then gradually tapers off. Some females have more testosterone than some males. The amount of testosterone can vary within a single individual practically from moment to moment. A person's emotional state will have an effect on the hormone's presence. For example, the thrill of winning a contest will increase the body's testosterone. Defeat will lower it.

The first role of testosterone is the determination of gender. Sometime during the second trimester of pregnancy one of the twenty-three chromosomes contained in human cells becomes an X plus Y combination thus forming a male fetus. Where the Y fails to appear there remains an X plus X chromosome that determines femaleness.

"Testosterone has many functions. Among other things, it signals cells to build muscle, make red blood cells, produce sperm, and release neurotransmitters in the brain."[91] It determines what we commonly call masculinity. It ·increases muscle bulk, causes the growth of body hair, lowers voice pitch, stimulates sexual drive, and much more. An important aspect of the "much more" are effects on mental functioning and overall behavior.

As I enumerate these characteristics, the reader must keep in mind that they are generalizations based on the vast range of variability among both sexes regarding testosterone levels.

The masculine mind is less adept in verbal skills. Attention has a more narrow range of focus. The Dabbs'[92] quote anthropologist Helen Fisher comparing female versus male thinking as "web thinking" contrasted with "step thinking." This reflects the idea that women have a broader awareness and see more connectedness in things than do males. Men take one

---

[91] Dabbs, James McBride and Dabbs, Mary Godwin. Hereos Rogues and Lovers: Testosterone and Behavior (New York: McGraw-Hill, 2000). P. 11.

[92] *Ibid.* P. 43.

thing at a time in a sequential manner. The testosterone driven individual's sense impressions are more vivid. They overcome problems rather than seek to understand them. The male has more formidable spatial skills and find direction by their sense of direction and distance. Females utilize landmarks to a greater extent.

Some of testosterone's effects on overall behavior are enumerated as follows. The overriding characteristic is the drive for dominance. This, of course, includes the need for control. The masculine person wants to be in charge. He wants to drive the car, decide what to do, command the conversation, and be the leader if at all possible. Competition is his world view. Another characteristic is the emphasis upon action. The tendency is, so to speak, to leap without looking. Testosterone fuels persistence which may lead to stubbornness. Non-conformity—not following the rules is also defining. Explosive temper is also a trait as is physical combativeness. High levels of testosterone leads to increased sex drive in both males and females. Such persons desire sex more frequently. They engage in more marital infidelity and have more sex partners from an early age on.

The above cited authors use the word "panache" to describe those endowed with high levels of testosterone. Panache means, according to Webster's dictionary, "a grand or flamboyant manner; verve; style; flair." Another descriptive word is "vanity." Such a trait is consistent with dominance and it serves to bluff others into thinking that he or she is the greatest. It's like Cassius Clay's declarations that served to intimidate his boxing opponents. It is the basis of body adornment such as tatoos, dyed hair, gold neck chains, ear rings, pierced body parts to accommodate jewelry, etc. Such extreme accouterments used to be pathognomonic of a psychopath. No longer. The psychopath has company with respect to showy style and self abuse.

The above cited authors have identified specific occupational groups who measure high in levels of testosterone. Leading the list are actors, followed by NFL football players, criminal trial lawyers, and blue collar workers in general as opposed to those working in white collar jobs.

Interestingly, of career women, the highest measured testosterone levels are for those working as trial lawyers.

The overly masculine male is likely to make a poor husband. He is not very concerned or perceptive of the needs of his family. He is not close emotionally to wife or children. The Dabbs' quote a characteristic comment "when I'm near the one I love, I love the one I'm near." In addition to being unfaithful and domineering, the male having a high level of testosterone is more apt to be an abuser. He is more prone to getting into fights with others, getting injured or killed, or ending up in jail. One positive aspect is that they are more likely to be altruistic heros if the opportunity presents itself.

Humans are not totally controlled by rampaging hormones. The function of the mind, a higher cortical process, has the potential for governing one's impulses and behaviors. That is what maturation, child development, education, role modeling, socialization, and moral training is about. High levels of testosterone may be contributory to deviant behavior. It could be one reason for the actions of such men as Nixon and Clinton but it cannot absolve them or others of their responsibilities. The next chapter will address possible solutions.

---

93 *Ibid.* P. 119.

CHAPTER VII

How Can We Reduce Stupidity?

The kind of stupidity we have been addressing is that shown by people we would regard as having at least normal intellectual potential. Since the potential is there, perhaps something can be done to unleash it. Recent investigations suggest that intellectual ability itself can be improved by learning new strategies related to thinking and problem solving. If this is so, one would think that the challenge of sharpening existing intellectual functioning should be readily achieved. Unfortunately, it isn't so easy.

Increase Motivation

The main reason for it not being easy has to do with a rather amorphous thing we call motivation. We think of motivation as being that stimulus or energy we experience as need, desire, want, or wish. These are aimed at a goal that is potentially satisfying. The source of what we call primary motivations or needs are biological. They relate to our survival as an organism and as a species. Included in the former is hunger and in the latter sex. There are secondary needs deriving their energy from being closely associated with a primary need. A strong interest and commitment to gourmet cooking is likely to rest on the shoulders of hunger. A

Casanova dedicated to his craft of pursuit and seduction would be nothing without his underlying sexual urges.

There appears to be tertiary needs we broadly ascribe to social learning. They don't seem to have any direct tie whatsoever with physiological needs. They are acquired but may be interactive with genetic predispositions. These tertiary motivations play a major role in human endeavors. Defining them has a certain arbitrariness because of the level of generalization one chooses. Fairly common generalized examples are the needs for acceptance, recognition, dominance, and achievement.

As noted we see these as learned though in part mediated by heredity. The process of learning in most cases probably begins early and progresses gradually. Social needs seem deeply ingrained once they take hold. In some instances they rule over basic biological instincts such as heroic altruism in defiance of death (there are those driven by a need for heroic action). Social motivations become what psychologists would refer to as ego syntonic, becoming part of oneself.

There are some identified tertiary needs that tend to make an individual more resistant to change under external pressure. A few are reviewed below.

1. Need for Superiority. This is most problematic when the emphasis is upon the use of power to control things, people, and ideas.

2. Need of Protectiveness. It is shown by an extraordinary effort to preserve one's self-respect and good name. Those driven by this need maintain a wall against criticism. They are highly sensitive over perceived personal slights.

3. Need for Asylum. This is characterized by wanting to avoid failure, shame, and humiliation to the point of not undertaking challenges.

4. Need of Defensiveness. This fires the motive to protect oneself against blame or deprecation. One is moved to offer excuses and justifications. The individual puts up a resistance to probing questions.

5. Need to Oppose. Someone so driven is determined to be contrary, to take the opposite view, to be different.

6. Need for Aggressiveness. This easily recognizable motivation is expressed by urges to ridicule, belittle, tease, be sadistic, and to physically assault.

Contrariwise, some tertiary motivations lead an individual to be more amenable to suggestions. A few are noted as follows.

1. Need for Achievement. This works when the outstanding feature of this need consists of striving to overcome difficult goals. The more that it reflects the need for power then the more problematic it becomes.

2. Need for Reflection and Inquiry. An insistence upon exercising the mind by raising questions and seeking knowledge. Curiosity. Careful observation, listening, and reading.

3. Need to Relate. This is unlike affiliation which is the near universal need to associate with others. It reveals itself in the desire to empathize and identify with others' concerns. It is shown by being open to suggestion and showing agreeableness.

4. Need to Shepherd. This is the desire to protect, help, aid, and nurture others.

There are other motives that fall in the middle and can go either way to aid or abet one's readiness to change. One that clearly stands out in this regard is the Need for Affirmation. It is the act of confirming or ratifying the fact that one exists. Descartes came close to missing the point when he declared "I think, therefore I am." An equally and perhaps more important observation is that "others affirm my thinking, therefore I must be."

Affirmation is what others do to us or for us. It is saying you are somebody deserving of notice. You matter. You are of some worth. Those not experiencing affirmation express the wish one way or another "notice me," "acknowledge me." They raise the question "don't I count?"

If there is cause for one to raise this question, then that someone may seek notice through positive or negative acts. If being my regular self, just being someone, goes without recognition then perhaps I should do something that can't be ignored. I could scale a dangerous cliff or ride my bicycle across country. On the other hand, I could go out and get stinking drunk. I could commit suicide. I could take a gun into school and shoot a lot of people.

Another example of an ambivalent sort of motivation is the Need of Deference. Someone driven by this motive is a willing follower. They readily identify with a leader and serve him loyally through thick and thin. The leader could be a Jimmy Carter or a James Jones. We most likely would regard the selection of the former leader as a wise choice and the latter as a stupid one.

For one to change requires a willingness to change. Such a willingness is akin to self-motivation. Most often successful change is not coerced but comes about because one sees how change will personally benefit him. He can also look at those things that he wants to change and find how they are in some way detrimental to his well being. Uncomfortable and distasteful things are a little easier to relinquish.

People don't change readily when they are under pressure. This happens whether the pressure is external or comes from within. Threat, fear, and anxiety, regardless of source, will diminish one's ability to change. Many who wish to change are already vulnerable to threat because they harbor feelings of guilt and shame. Some have assumed a particular ideological stance because of deep underlying insecurities. A frontal, verbal attack against their belief system is likely only to increase resistence to change. They get into a defensive mode and harden their position. Their defense may take the form of a vigorous offense.

During the years of the fifties and sixties when civil rights issues were in the forefront, the assertion was frequently made that attitudes and morals couldn't be legislated. The assumption was that for people to alter their behavior basic beliefs had to change. The assertion concerning attitudes and morals was correct but the assumption about change was wrong. Legislation and court rulings did change behavior. Subsequently, we discovered that when the behavior changed, attitudes and morals began to change in a majority of people. Racial prejudice did not evaporate from all of society but it did moderate in most and it practically disappeared in some (unfortunately it may have intensified in a few).

Change may be facilitated from an external source when strong leaders, whether politicians, spiritual guides, or secular authorities, vigorously espouse the need for specific changes. If the majority of major media sources, pull together and consistently promote a particular cause it is likely to be realized.

Self-motivation can come from the process of discovering for oneself the reasons for making a change. It is usually more effective when positive features are emphasized. One can set goals, become active in achieving them, and then provide self-rewards as there is notable progress. Outsiders can be helpful by serving as consultants. They do so by providing factual knowledge and information about proven aids for success. As a consultant they are non-judgmental. What follows may serve in part as a consultant's manual.

Cultivate a Critical Attitude

Foremost is consideration of what I call a critical attitude. There should be a mind set for monitoring and evaluating novelty and old things that no longer work. It is as though we have a guardian that sits at the portal of consciousness and checks on what seeks to enter. This would include what we refer to as sensations, perceptions, facts, and concepts.

Granted, there are a lot of ways and occasions when we operate on automatic. Things go on mentally that don't seem to pass by our conscious awareness. That is as it should be and must be. Though our brains appear to be the seat of mind, most of what we call mental processing occurs in that part of the brain called the cerebral cortex. It envelops the top portion of the brain just beneath the top of our skull. It is the most recent product of evolutionary development within the central nervous system. Thus we tend to refer to it as "higher order" functioning. It is high on the evolutionary scale, high in the sense of lying on top of the brain, and high in level of complexity.

There is a progression downward from the cerebral cortex to other morphological structures of the brain that have progressively more primitive functions. That is, they are deemed primitive because they came earlier on the evolutionary scale and they mediate basic biological processes. Included are breathing, heart beat, temperature control, hunger, thirst, and sexual urges. Included also, is an alert system that prepares us to respond to emergencies. Our senses and perceptual abilities are in an operating mode even when cognitive functions can't be brought into play. We are enabled to apply the automobile brakes in the presence of a threat without conscious thinking. Commonly, there is no time for that.

What emerges and operates from the sub-cortex is often regarded as instinctual. It is like neurons are hard wired so as to function in a particular way. It is like what we can rely on for consistency. We normally breathe without thinking. We don't have to contemplate our pulse rate. However, these and other normally reflexive actions can be consciously manipulated. We can alter our breathing and pulse rates at will if we so choose. We can also increase our awareness of sensations. Frequently we find ourselves eating food such as an orange and not really savoring its taste. We can relish the sweetness, juiciness, and texture more if we set our minds to it. The same applies to our various other senses.

Attention, awareness, and cognitive processing is what we need in exercising a critical attitude. Being like the man from Missouri is facilitating, the man who insists on "show me." We might also follow the lead of Detective Friday who persistently asks "just tell me the facts Mam." There is an important place for constructive skepticism.

Fortunate are those blessed with an inquisitive mind. They have a mind-set to seek evidence whether pro or con about assertions of fact or declarations about infallible truths. Open up to the realm of possibilities. Let your mind follow every lead. It can be vitally important to avoid making stupid mistakes. Such mistakes can have dire consequences for the individual and society.

Hone Skills of Logic and Systematic Reasoning

Previous chapters have addressed the subjects of deductive and inductive logic and scientific analysis. Most of us have not had formal instruction in them. However, we have absorbed a great deal from our modern culture, well characterized as the age of science and discovery. Some of what we have absorbed has to do with approaches to problem solving. An effective place to start is to define the problem facing us. We need to define it in such a way that in seeking answers we will come up with a result bearing on the problem. First and foremost we must have a vocabulary that is ultimately referenced in reality. The vocabulary must be unambiguous and consistent in its usage. We must be able to understand the language employed and agree on its meaning. Interestingly at times, when a workable vocabulary is developed, a good deal of the problem may be solved.

A problem once defined raises one or more questions whose answers we seek in a series of observations from relevant experiences. A problem for us might be to explain the results of the 2000 presidential election. It might boil down to why did Al Gore not win. His not winning was the result of not gaining enough electoral votes, a majority was needed He received a total of 266, five short of George W. Bush's 271. If Gore had won any other state he would have won the presidency (his popular vote count exceeded Bush's by 539, 947 votes). Of course, the Florida outcome was the final determining factor. In that decision the question remains as to whether minorities in that state were unfairly excluded from having their votes counted. Speculation is that if they had been, Gore would have won Florida and thus the election.

There were three other states that Gore was expected to win based on tradition. They were Arkansas, Tennessee, and West Virginia. Arkansas was Bill Clinton's home state and Gore, as his Vice-President, should have had an edge. Fifty-one percent of that state's vote went to Bush. In other contests three of four house seats went to democrats. The state cast six electoral votes.

Tennessee was Gore's home state. He had represented that state in the house and senate for many years before assuming the Vice-Presidency. Bush got fifty-one percent of its vote. Other contests included one in the senate that went to a republican. There were nine house seats contested and only four went to democrats. Tennessee had eleven electoral votes.

West Virginia was traditionally a democratic state. Bush received fifty-two percent of the vote. Other state contests included the governorship. It went to a democrat. The only contested senate seat went to a democrat. Two of three house seats went to democrats. West Virginia had five electoral votes.

An explanation of these results can be had by an analysis of exit polls. Scientific surveys would also provide an answer. Speculation that could qualify as hypotheses was that Gore went too far left of center. His support of gun control, opposition to the tobacco lobby, and pro-life stance led to his defeat in each of the three states.

Following such a line of investigation does not offer scientific proof. It only offers a plausible explanation based on observable evidence rather than off-handed guessing.

Develop the Full Range of Your Cognitive Potential

In Chapter I, reference was made to multiple factors relating to intellectual abilities. The traditional thesis had been that intelligence was essentially what IQ tests measured. That notion is dangerously misleading. The content of IQ tests focus upon linguistic and logical-mathematical aptitudes. These happen to be the foundation of our formal school curriculums from kindergarten through university graduate school.

Academic success is largely determined by how well students do in these two realms of cognitive functioning. Strength in these areas, however, are only moderately correlated with achievement in college and in future careers. The conclusion should be obvious that much more goes into insuring success in life. Some of the *more* appears to be additional types of cognitive skills.

Psychologist, educator, and specialist in neurology, Howard Gardner[94], has for some twenty years been researching his theory of multiple intelligences. Whether or not the six new, additional intelligences he proposes are each a separate identifiable intelligence, the abilities described obviously play an important role in cognition. Nevertheless, he builds a very strong evidentiary case that each is deserving to be labeled an intelligence. They are as follows: musical, bodily-kinesthetic, spatial, interpersonal, intrapersonal, and naturalist intelligences. All people manifest some capacity for each kind of intelligence. They all show some variation in strength in each so that they have a unique profile of cognitive abilities. Typically, an individual shows notable strengths in as many as three areas.

When relative weaknesses are identified, it is possible to improve upon them. Women on average seem to be less endowed with spatial intelligence than are the average male. Given special instruction, training, and practice women have a meaningful increased gain in performing spatial tasks or solving problems involving spatial intelligence. The average man is commonly regarded as being less adept with interpersonal relations than is the average women. Men have been aided in such a way as to significantly improve their interpersonal intelligence. Naturalist intelligence does not seem to reflect a gender difference. This kind of intelligence has to do primarily with recognition and classification of the things of this world. Biologists, botanists, entomologists, and pathologists clearly represent those ranking high in this form of intelligence. Organizational and

---

[94] Gardner, Howard. Intelligence Reframed: Multiple Intelligences for the 21st Century (New York: Basic Books, 1999).

systematizing behaviors associated with naturalist intelligence can be acquired. Thus it goes, the odds are that any particular intellectual ability can be improved by special attention. This broadening effect may be critical in avoiding serious acts of stupidity.

Develop the Shadow Side of Your Personality

In the introduction, reference was made to Carl Jung's idea of our having a dark side to our personalities. It was said then that it was every bit as important to look at this dark side as to focus upon the positive enhancement of our evident strengths. Jung referred to this darkness as falling within our shadow side. A well known Jungian analyst, Robert A. Johnson[95], has expounded upon this phenomena in his book titled *Owning Your Own Shadow.* He describes its origin, nature, and function in human experience.

Consistent with Johnson, my view is that the shadow originates as a function of acculturation. In my way of thinking, we humans like most higher order mammals, come into being with a number of instinctual drives and a range of possibilities for individual diversity. We are not fully equipped to survive on our own. We are not like the giant sea turtle that emerges from its egg and immediately scrambles into the ocean to survive or not, largely by chance. Instead we mammals encounter the natural world under the tutelage of adults of our species, particularly our parents. We must learn from them how to function within a community and meet the challenges of everyday life as it is and as it unfolds. Failure in receiving nurturing, instruction, and training is likely to result in total dependence and probable premature death. The *Free Willy* story is a fair illustration of what happens to a mammal deprived of its normal environment and

---

[95] Johnson, Robert A. Owning Your Own Shadow: Understanding the Dark Side of the Psyche (New York: HarperCollins, 1993).

learning opportunities. The true Willy character, an orca, once liberated is still unable to fend on its own after years of trying to acclimate to the ocean environment.

Human's maturation is accompanied by a process identified as acculturation. We acquire skills to cope with life's challenges. We also are taught to squelch certain impulses and desires that those around us regard as detrimental to ourselves or the greater good and well being of the group. What is squelched might be valid for the time and circumstance but it might also be arbitrary. Those parts of ourselves that were once conscious and are then rejected do not leave us. They are tucked away somewhere within the depths of our minds, in a realm commonly referred to as the unconscious. They are cast away directly under the pressure of others or by ourselves under indirect pressures issuing from such processes as conscience or super-ego. The shadows have as much or more energy than does the functioning ego.

Johnson writes of the gold that lies within the shadows. Every component of the unconscious is not in itself negative or destructive. If given direct expression as in an impulsive act, some repressed material can appear prosaic or miraculous. I have long argued that every impulsive act is not calamitous. In fact, a leap into raging waters to save a drowning person, truly executed on impulse, is a selfless, heroic act.

The extensive list of positive values generated by Johnson,[96] have polar opposites. There is, for example, winning and losing, action and passivity, and freedom and obedience. There is also life and death and love versus hate. The polarities make up our reality. Most appear to be irreconcilable and in conflict. They need not be. They, in fact, must not always be separate. Johnson would like for us to have the insight to recognize and understand the paradoxical nature of these polarities. Paradox is to be defined according to Webster's prime meaning: "a statement or proposition that seems self-contradictory or absurd but in reality expresses a possible

---

[96] *Ibid.* P. 78-79.

truth." The strictly obedient child has a shadow side containing urges toward freedom. The lover knows of hate within his mind's shadow. The religious person affirming life has a shadow image of death. These polarities coexist and complete the person. Particularly, when recognized and integrated within consciousness, they cause a person to become rational and fully human. The unrecognized and unacknowledged shadow side of our psyche may permit such things as anxiety, fear, and hate to control our actions. They can function as separate entities unmodified, unfiltered by their paradoxical elements of quiescence, courage, and love. Opening ourselves to our shadow side requires both insight and courage. If we are to escape from stupidity both individually and collectively, we must come go grips with ourselves at this level of reality.

Learn to Recognize the Authoritarian Personality

Authoritarianism has long been a part of the human scene. We know not when it began. Probably, it stemmed from our primitive ancestors living in small familial groups under the absolute command of the strongest and perhaps wisest member. Such an individual was most likely to be the male progenitor of the principle family group. This leadership arrangement likely had considerable survival value in primitive society. Somewhere along the evolutionary time-line other models of political organization emerged. Chances are that all too many times the powerful leader was anything but benevolent, just, and effective. If so, the group may have risen up and asserted its will to replace the leader with another or to devise a new way to execute the functioning of the group. Here, then, was a distinction between authority and authoritarianism. Time has proved that absolute authority vested in one or a few persons will result in oppression and ruthless tyranny, this to the detriment of vast numbers of people.

Modern history exemplifies this in the person of Adolph Hitler. This dictator was a ruthless tyrant. How could he have emerged from what was then viewed as the most Christian and civilized nation in the world? The answer is a complex one but what is important is that he did emerge there. In 1932 the Nazi party was elected to a majority of seats in the Reichstag. The following year Hitler was granted dictatorial powers. Behind the persona of the German people were feelings of resentment, anxiety, fear, and hatred. These feelings were exploited by a demagogue of a man. He became the Fuhrer—the Leader. He led the world to destruction.

The existence of this man prompted behavioral scientists in the 1940's to study the authoritarian personality. It was their hope that by recognizing and understanding it they could somehow ameliorate its effects. Could one possessing such personality traits change? Could people learn to recognize such individuals and be able to resist their appeals to our base nature?

The early studies focused on fascism and anti-Semitism. It became clear that bigotry, ethnocentrism, and political conservatism correlated highly with measures of fascism. Those expressing anti-Semitism tended to be equally prejudiced toward other targeted groups such as blacks and homosexuals. Further study indicated that the authoritarianism undergirding fascism was a far more general trait than fascism alone. The authoritarian personality was revealed within the full political spectrum from the extreme right to the radical left and all points in between. Such personalities could be found in arenas other than the political. They could be in journalism, religion, science and so on. An important distinction was then made between content and structure of belief systems to find the common underlying element of authoritarianism. Specific content of beliefs was not a distinguishing feature. One could be pro-choice and not be an open-minded liberal. Such a one might dogmatically and rigidly adhere to his pro-choice stance. Rather than the particular belief or ideology, it was the manner in which the individual justified and defended his point of view. In other words, it was the structure of his thought processes.

Authoritarianism rests upon a host of traits. Included are usurping power, being opinionated, acting in a judgmental fashion, asserting intolerance, expressing bigotry, manifesting closed-mindedness, lacking patience, avoiding criticism, and desiring exclusivity in relationships. The latter is expressed by associating only with those who are acquiescent or who appear to be in agreement with oneself. The authoritarian personality is likely to be narrow of mind, rigid, and bombastic in expressing and defending his position. The slightest frustration may lead to an eruption of anger. If one were to offend this sort, don't expect forgiveness and acceptance. Because the authoritarian personality shuts himself off from the opinion and advice of others, thus narrowing his focus and restricting his cognitive field, he should not be counted on to make rational choices. Regardless of his motives or good intentions, regardless of his supreme confidence, regardless of regalness, he is likely to be a dangerous man.

Become the CEO of Your Own Experiences

The preceding section addressed the dangers of the authoritarian personality. Here we examine the need for the individual serving as his own locus of authority. I characterize this as becoming a CEO (Chief Executive Officer) of your own life. The basic tenant of western society has for centuries been the autonomy of the individual. It is difficult to push its historical roots further back in history than the Greek philosopher Plato (428-347 B.C.E.). Plato's emphasis upon ideal forms of being as the true reality opposed to the physical reality of our everyday experience set the stage for individualism. Discovery of the nature of Plato's ideal was by way of logical reasoning and intuition. He believed that only a few individuals, notably philosophers, were capable of knowing ideal reality. We can leap forward over a thousand years to the ideas of St. Thomas Aquinas (1225-1274 C.E.) to see the fruits of Platonist thinking. For Aquinas, the measure of human action depended upon the individual's relationship to divine truth rather than on societal standards. Aquinas believed in "eternal laws" and "right reason" that existed apart from ordinary human affairs. Moral judgments depended upon an individual's relationship to God.

Predating Plato, who opposed democracy, was Solon who laid the foundations for a democratic Athens in 594 B.C.E. This form of government, so laudable in this modern day, has nearly become the universal ideal. Its foundation rests upon individual freedom and equality. Our democratic judicial system's primary principle is to protect the rights of individuals. Our capitalist economic system also is enmeshed with individual persons acting autonomously.

The preeminence of individual will appears set against collectivism. Might there be a clash between the rights of an individual and those of the larger society? Certainly this commonly occurs. The freedom of one person may be opposed to the freedom of even one other person. When it does we must turn to the rule of law. A recent example of this occurred in the State of Vermont. A farmer there had a few years previously imported a herd of several hundred sheep from Belgium. It was determined that those sheep may have been exposed to mad cow disease. If so they would present a catastrophic threat to the entire livestock industry in this country and to the survival of humans who might later consume meat products from infected animals. The government ordered a quarantine of the sheep herd and later demanded confiscation and subsequent slaughter of the animals. The farmer refused to cooperate and took his case to court. He lost his case, appealed, and lost again. The courts weighed the individual's loss against the potential horrific loss to society as a whole. One man's rights were measured against those of many others.

One way of approaching the potential conflict between the rights of two or more people is to exercise the golden rule: "do unto others as you would have them do unto you." Too much "me-ism" in society can lead to chaos. Endless competition can lead to a deadly divisiveness. Competition at the expense of cooperation can be a terrible barrier to progress.

All of the preceding harangue about the individual and society bears upon the philosophical basis of the CEO concept. Individuals must become their own chief executive. This means that they should not relinquish their right to decide for themselves. They are to be held responsible for their decisions. They are to suffer the consequences for wrong decisions and receive credit for the right ones. Autonomy is maintained. However, management consultants have looked at the styles of successful CEO's. They found that in addition to their responsible sense of personal authority, good CEO's were keenly attuned to the needs of their employees and their customers. They set up a positive atmosphere within the work place, built team spirit, encouraged group decision making, delegated responsibility, and built incentives to reward productivity. Being your own CEO is to be responsible to yourself and to one's larger society. This is a neat blend of two apparent polarities. It reflects the paradox described above under the heading of one's shadow side, a paradox whose resolution is a larger truth.

Understand (and Be Forewarned About) the Mental Mechanisms

The concept of defense or adjustment mechanisms were discussed and described in some detail in Chapter VI. Critical to the theory is that these psychic functions have their source in the unconscious. The unconscious was described above as the shadow side of our mentation. We must realize that there are potent forces within our personalities besides biological drives and habituation. Such forces can lead to irrational decisions and actions.

A little bit of the how of owning one's own shadow side is in understanding the details of the mental mechanisms. Understanding them facilitates recognizing them when they are at play in our everyday life. A capacity for introspection is beneficial for identifying motives and thoughts that are beneath ordinary awareness. Thus identified we can gain conscious control of them.

Thompson[97] referred to casting our shadow self on other people. It is a failure in owning one's own shadow. It happens frequently and it is very destructive of both oneself and the other person. This "casting" phenomena is a function of the mental mechanism of projection.

Projection as described earlier plays a part in other defense mechanisms and it may be seen in individuals we would deem as normal. However, it can be very serious because of frequency and duration of use and its near total disregard of reality. Projection may achieve the level of delusion and it may undergird the content of hallucinations. In these instances it is clearly recognizable as irrational.

Projection serves as a defense against anxiety by casting unacceptable attitudes, traits, and motives within oneself onto others. One of the most common examples in present day society is homophobia. Webster's definition of homophobia is an "unreasoning fear of or antipathy toward homosexuals and homosexuality." One who simply declares that he does not approve of homosexuality would not be manifesting homophobia. The definition hinges on the phrase "unreasoning fear or antipathy." Why would one respond with such intense negative emotions toward other people's life style? In what manner is the homosexual such a threat?

Pollack[98] documents how extensive fears of homosexuality occupies the minds of adolescent males. They are more fearful of their peers taunting them about being gay than they are of those identified as being homosexual. Pollack writes of the "boy code" which includes being an emotionless, viral, heterosexual male. Those who can't keep up this image are vulnerable to cruel teasing and other forms of hazing. What of the brazen macho type? Why so forward in asserting his masculinity? This brings to mind the quotation "me thinks thou protestest too much." Perhaps alarmingly, the answer lies in repressed homosexual urges. Biologically both sexes have significant amounts of male and female hormones. Taoist philosophy

---

[97] *Op Cite.* Thompson. Pp. 32, 34, 46.
[98] Pollack, William S. Real Boy's Voices (New York: Random House, 2000).

addresses the Yin and Yang each of us has. Yin is female and in part characterized by earth. Yang is male and it is partly characterized by fire. The blending of one's Yin and Yang yields harmony. Males hopefully will be in touch with some of the Yin within themselves. Among them might be the commonly identified feminine traits of emotional expressiveness, connection with others, tenderness, and circumspection.

The homophobic male is projecting his shocking repressed attraction to other males on to others. His urge is kept from consciousness and is instead attributed to another. The homophobic boy or man could not stand being the perceived object of another male's lust. His repugnance and hostility masks the very impulses lying within himself. He becomes blind to both inner and outer realities. An appreciation of the underlying dynamics of his homophobia proves him to be the klutz that he is.

Avoid Linguistic and Semantic Traps

Chapter V contains a detailed discussion of problems falling within the linguistic field of knowledge. Some of this discussion contained suggestions of how to rectify linguistic errors. Here I will touch upon some of the highlights since they play such a critical roll in propelling smart people along paths marked by stupidity.

The problems lie in three broad areas. One is our thought processes. Two is the manner of expression each of us uses to achieve our own ends. Third is our being able to sort out the meanings others are trying to convey to us. Language is a vital tool of our existence. We must learn how to use it well in our thinking, in our expressing ourselves, and in receiving information from others. We have the capacity and opportunity to control each of these types of language applications.

The components of language such as words, phrases, sentences, narratives, and so on, are the products of human beings. They are symbolic of something concrete in our environment or of some ideas we have identified by employing other symbols. The language we use is not the things in themselves. If I take an ice cube from the refrigerator and it melts, I no longer have the three dimensional object of frozen water. However, I still have the word "ice cube" and I can describe its defining characteristics. The word and the thing it names aren't the same. The lake that suddenly appears before the eyes of a desert traveler turns out not to be a lake. One can't drink the water from such a lake because it is a mirage. One nearly dead of thirst would have desperately desired for the word to have been the thing itself containing potable water.

Because of the symbolic nature of our language, we can never know with absolute certainty the "true" meaning of any human expression. No one is ever going to get inside of another person's mind to divine intent or apprehension. If I were to declare to my spouse that I have a sore foot, she wouldn't have learned very much. In all likelihood, because she cares, she would say that she was sorry to hear that I was experiencing discomfort. She would likely follow-up with questions such as "how did you hurt it?" Which foot is it? Where on your foot? There could be many further questions and informative responses. The initial declaration failed to say a lot of things. To begin with what was my reason for mentioning it? Did I want her sympathy? Did I want her assistance? How bad did it hurt? Was it disabling? Such questions could go on and on. However, she would never know the true nature or extent of my pain and anxiety. She would never know whether I genuinely was comforted by her response and so on.

With the subjective world of another, you can get closer and closer in understanding its nature by obtaining more clues. You can go far in stepping into his shoes by relying on your knowledge and particularly by the application of intuition and empathy. But you will never gain absolute certainty about his subjective experience. If he has a modicum of practical sense, he will know that you can't totally understand. However, there is a recognizable point when the two of you reach good-enough agreement. In human interactions anyway, it is the commitment to achieve understanding that matters above all else.

In the realm of human sensations, there can be no argument. I say the room is too warm. My wife says it is too cold. "The TV is too loud. No! I can barely hear it." Who is correct. Some years ago two astronomers were making careful observations of some astronomical events. They discovered that in spite of looking at the same phenomena they were reporting the results differently. Further inquiry revealed that they had different reaction times. This was based upon a difference in their physiology, probably an innate difference. Such discrepancies between people's experiences should not lead to disputes.

Another type of futile argument between people concerns matters of fact that can be checked out. One man contends that the Baltimore Ravens NFL team won the 2001 Super Bowl. Another claims that it was the New York Giants. They fight about it. Before a fight starts why not say "hold on a minute, let's check the record to determine the actual result." I have witnessed many arguments over such things as the dates of prior events. Disagreements could easily be put on hold until the facts are checked. Not doing so is utterly stupid.

As mentioned in Chapter V, making assertions in absolute terminology raises the ire of most listeners. This is because few things in life are black or white, either/or. Human experience comes in shades of gray. How silly it is when one raises his voice to get his point of view across. How can he believe that loudness is evidence of reason? All that the loudness proves is how strong one feels over the issue itself or how important it is to win the argument. Bullying is not nice and it is stupid.

People have differing tastes and values. There are adult males who wear their hair in long braids. Young females put rings in their noses. Adolescents dye their hair hideous colors. Are these legitimate sources of contention? No! These are issues of taste. They are no different from the fact that I like pistachio flavored ice cream. My wife would prefer butter pecan. So what.

What of differences in personal values? I have a neighbor who wouldn't be caught dead driving any car other than a Mercedes. I am a Dodge man myself. We still get along with one another. I have another neighbor who is Jewish and still another who is Catholic. Both take their respective faiths seriously as I take my Protestant beliefs. We aren't in contention with one another over these matters of belief. I would describe myself as being politically liberal. When I act from this perspective, I espouse various values. For example, I support holding HMO's more accountable to their clients. I believe in lowering the standards for blood-alcohol levels to determine whether or not a person is driving under the influence of intoxicants. I believe in government funding of overseas family planning clinics. I presume that conservatives I might encounter would discuss such value differences in a civil and intelligent manner. I can find no logical or moral grounds for them to burn crosses on my lawn, smash my mail box, or harass my children because of our conflict in values.

It is important to recognize that there are many and continuing efforts being made to impact our decision making processes. This is OK. My wife from time-to-time will try to get me to go to the movies with her. Sometimes I yield to her reasoning, sometimes I don't. Advertisers try to sell me various products. They bring to my attention the merits of what they have to sell. I can take it or leave it. Political candidates seek my vote by sending me letters and appearing on TV during the time ordinarily devoted to commercials. No problem. I can throw the letters in the trash, turn to another TV channel, or better yet head for the bathroom.

What is not OK and why we should be aware is that potential persuaders and influence peddlers commonly resort to dishonest use of language. Obviously, they can tell very clever lies. We have to be careful where we place our trust. We need to develop useful standards for judging integrity

We need to recognize linguistic tricks when they are being employed. For example, when told not to vote for a certain political candidate because of his voting record on tobacco issues twenty years ago, we should question whether it is really true and if so where does the candidate stand on that issue now. An argument against a candidate might go as follows:

"he was a friend of so-and-so who was employed by such and such a business, and you know the product they make." This is a hearsay argument and an appeal for guilt by association. A candidate makes a claim for a prior success which, in fact, was in no way successful. Politicians do such things because the odds are great that only a few will challenge the statement's accuracy. False claims is an extremely common practice with the promotion of consumer products. It was the standard pitch for the old snake oil remedy. It is now common to hear the phrase "science proves" this or that. It's still the snake oil scam.

Name calling, belittling, ridiculing, and so on are not rational arguments. We should not allow ourselves to be persuaded by them.

Coercion is often used from the lesser force of the necessity of keeping up with the Jones' to the greater one of not being worthy of belonging. A further escalation might be in hearing that you are going to hell if you don't do as I ask. The last straw might be to have some of your privileges removed.

If you are looking for further remedies regarding linguistic tricks, you may review the beginning of Chapter V.

Improve Communication Skills

I recall reading some years ago of the need for an eleventh commandment. It was suggested to be that "thou shalt not remain silent." The notion had profound meaning to me. This was probably because I could recall a number of instances in my own past when there was a situation crying for something to be said and I didn't say it. It was the kind of occasion when one would say that "the silence was deadening." It could be either an opportunity missed to ease someone's concerns or the silence alone conveyed a rejection. Sometimes the needed words might have been a simple "I'm sorry," "I understand," "you have my sympathy, or "I appreciate what you did." At other times it may have been more complicated such as "I sense there is something troubling you. Do you want to talk about it?"

In all human relationships, open channels of communication have to be maintained. There are no viable alternatives. Presently, there is much talk about violence among youth. We have experienced all too many tragedies of young people resorting to guns and bombs to destroy other's lives. There has been a great deal of speculation as to why such things occur. Many likely causative factors have emerged. But the single most significant factor is a lack of connectedness. Too many young people feel isolated (and they probably are). They don't feel that there is anyone they can turn to, make a connection with, and trust. They feel distant from their parents, their siblings if they have any, their peers, neighbors, and others within their normal surroundings. This lack of connectedness is the result of a lack of genuine communication. They have no one with whom they can comfortably, freely open up and express their deepest concerns. Significant people in their lives have too often shut the door to discourse or they have allowed the door to remain closed. Consider the eleventh commandment. Thou shalt not remain silent.

All of our utterances are an expression of a need. When we think we have something to say or to write, we should be in touch with the specific, momentary, operating need. Doing so will facilitate the expression of a clear and direct message. A simple example is to be among a group of people. Not having a watch or clock available and desiring to know the time, you announce to anyone within hearing "I wonder what time it is." Chances are you will get the response you desire. However, you will have greater assurance of getting the desired answer if you were to address the question "Can any of you tell me the time?" Think of the many occasions when two friends are together and one asks the other "what should we do?" And the response is "I don't know. What would you like to do?" So it goes on, perhaps with one finally saying "well, I asked you first." Chances are neither is being honest. For one reason or another they do not choose to state their need or want. Say what you want. A discussion will ensue and a decision will be made. Vagueness and circumlocutions have no place in effective communication.

In 1970 I attended a week long workshop in Boston conducted by Dr. Thomas Gordon. The subject matter was what he called "Parent Effectiveness Training." I chose to attend because of my interest in helping children in my professional practice and to better relate to my own daughters. I had studied and thought a great deal about how to talk with children. I had previously read the books of Heim Ginot and attended one of his stimulating and enlightening lectures. His notion of the need to learn the language of "childrenese" both amused me and awakened me to the fact that there was something different in communicating with children. Not being satisfied with my skills in this area, I welcomed Dr. Gordon's course.

To the best of my knowledge, no one had previously devised such a coherent, systematic, practical, and meaningful approach to the learning of interpersonal language skills as had Dr. Gordon. I have since seen many variants of his approach. I have seen some of his innovations become commonplace when there is talk about communication. It was soon obvious that most of his principles applied equally as well to adults as to children.

Dr. Gordon, who had been a student of Dr. Carl Rogers while at the University of Chicago, pointed out that parents are "blamed not trained." Parents as well as everyone else aren't given formal instruction on how to communicate effectively. Isn't it a wonder why this is so? Something of such great importance is left to hit and miss conditioning. Dr. Gordon launched a nationwide training program for parents. Later it was extended to teachers and then soon followed for an even wider consumer group. His program offered ample evidence that effective communication skills can be taught.

I will describe briefly a few of his major topics to give the flavor of the skill training. Early in his course, students learn about common pitfalls that stand in the way of constructive communication. He listed them in twelve categories he referred to as roadblocks. (My class promptly identified them as "the dirty dozen."). One such category by way of illustration was "name-calling, ridiculing, shaming." Such remarks give the listener an odious label and injures his self-esteem. A second category is identified as "exhorting, moralizing, preaching." The "you should" and the "you ought" remarks are belittling.

Dr. Gordon compared two classes of statements. One was called "you messages" and the other "I messages." When someone does something that makes you uncomfortable, it is commonplace to offer a remark beginning with the personal pronoun "you." It might take the form of "you are trying your best to annoy me." Such a response is unlikely to enlist the other's goodwill and cooperation. On the other hand, one might say "I am finding it difficult to concentrate on my reading when the radio is turned up so loudly." In this case, their is no accusation. The comment tells of your need and how it is being interfered with. Implied in the statement is that the reading activity is of some substantial importance to you, such as preparing for an assignment. The odds are that the latter approach will lead to a quick, simple, and amicable solution. Though this sounds like a stylized formula, it serves only as a model.

Dr. Gordon should be credited with the expression "active listening." It is to be differentiated from passive listening where there is no response when remarks are made. It is different also from non-verbal nods or shakes of the head and different from grunts and uh-huh's. These may have their place in normal conversation but they fail to convey to the speaker that he is being understood. The significance of active listening is best understood by way of a communication paradigm illustrating feedback. The speaker's message is encoded and sent. The listener hears it, decodes it, and replies (gives feedback) in such a way that it demonstrates understanding both at the content level and the emotional level. The reply must be genuine and not a simple parroting.

Another critical topic in Dr. Gordon's class is one relating to conflict resolution. His is a win-win method that goes beyond compromise. It involves defining the problem, exploring creative proposals to find a reso-lution, evaluating the various ideas, deciding on a particular solution, agreeing upon a strategy of implementation, and periodically conducting a follow-up evaluation. If it isn't working, go back to step one.

Effective communication must rest upon mutual respect. This means that each person's needs must be taken into consideration. It is obvious that communication gets no-where if it is one-sided.

Create Safeguards Against Chancy Behavior

We cannot go through life without taking chances. For one thing, we were not granted the attribute of omniscience. We can't see around corners or otherwise foresee future events. The future is apparently not fixed or preordained. Causal determinism, though having a significant roll in the unfolding of events, can't account for chance happenings.

I doubt that a serious person would want it any other way. It would be nice under certain circumstances to tell in advance what is going to hap-pen. A case in point is a day spent at the race track or on the casino floor among banks of slot machines. However, otherwise life would be very bor-ing if you always knew ahead of time what was going to happen next. The excitement of anticipation would be gone as would be the challenge.

The famous, near modern day philosopher, Alfred North Whitehead, advanced the importance of adventure in human activity. Though he was not specifically thinking of wrestling alligators or climbing mountains, what he was thinking of was inclusive of such acts but went far beyond them. He was thinking of the unleashing of the human imagination. Van Wesep[101] writes that Whitehead viewed the adventurous man not being

---

[101] Van Wesep, H. B. Seven Sages: The Story of American Philosophy (New York: Longmans, Green and Co., 1960). P. 431.

afraid of what is new but instead being eager to look forward to see if there might be something that could be put to use. Whitehead's world view gave the realm of possibilities a prominent place. Adventure led to new possibilities. The acting upon man's spirit for venturing into new places and new spheres of thought required courage.

The world being how it is, we have to take chances whether we like it or not. Staying in bed all day has its debilitating risks. We go forth to take on challenges in every day living as well as pushing ahead to try the extraordinary. Why do we do so? It may be in the sense that Whitehead's philosophy suggests—it could be in our genes. Pushing into the unknown certainly has survival benefits with respect to our species. It could be for purposes of relieving us of boredom. It could be from the joy of discovery and accomplishment. We might see it as an affirmation of self, proving that one could do it. The experience of adventure could simply contain the excitement of life's unfolding. Of course, there may be things to gain. One might receive public acclaim—be called a hero. One might receive a trophy or money. Adventure could lead to discovery such as gaining important new knowledge. It could advance the welfare of the human community.

The message is take chances. Don't turn away from challenges. Open your eyes to the future. Take hold of some of the promising possibilities that will be revealed.

There are, however, cautions one must consider. In Chapter IV, risk takers were discussed. A principle point was to make a wise assessment of the degree of risk versus the potential benefit. A second principle was that adequate preparation was often required. This could involve training, supervision, and proper outfitting.

Above all other considerations, one must make a distinction as to whether he is testing himself or testing fate. The former keeps one in reality. The latter places one in the surreal. The man who sky dives from a cliff with the thought in mind that he is putting himself in the hands of fate to prove his worthiness or something of that nature, is a foolish man. It's not the way to establish whether or not God accepts you or loves you. The risk taker must not cast away his rationality.

Revitalize Education

Education with respect to the school experience that our children and youth receive is getting considerable attention at this time—the time of George W. Bush's first year as president. Many proposals are being entertained such as public funding of private schools and yearly standardized testing to evaluate children's degree of academic progress. It also has been proposed to periodically administer standard testing of teachers to determine their teaching competence.

Our educational system needs reform. The heavy emphasis upon formal testing is not the way to go. The types of tests available are in themselves unreliable and of questionable validity. The means of administering, scoring, and interpreting them are far from being controlled in such a manner that they will yield meaningful results.

The population of school children are far from being homogeneous and they cannot all be assessed in the same manner.

When there is so much emphasis placed upon test scores—scores by which the student is evaluated along with the teacher, school, school district, and state—the test will dictate the curriculum and pedagogical approach in the classroom. Cheating will occur as it has in a number of comparable situations. Low achieving students are encouraged to stay home on test days so as not to lower average scores. Underachievers are counseled to drop out of school. Teachers give students answers to test questions in advance. Teachers and principals falsify the test scores in order to improve upon the average. To believe that the threat of expulsion and more drastic punishment will deter such abuses is naive. Some form of policing would be required to insure compliance to rules. Such is unacceptable.

How are we to determine whether our children are learning what they should when they should? The answer cries out loud and clear. We have to have effective teaching. The competent, well functioning teacher will optimize the learning their children acquire. They will know that their children know. They will know because they make assessments on a daily basis. They employ the technique of performance of understanding. The child is given a multiplicity of opportunities to show they have the required knowledge and skills. Teachers who make assessments in this way focus upon the individual child in a non-threatening manner. The unspoken message to the child is that you will have all the help you need and many creative opportunities to demonstrate that you are learning. You don't fail. You have more possibilities for success.

I will deal with teachers in a moment. First, look at the curriculum. Granted, we must teach the traditional academic subjects such as reading, writing, arithmetic, history, social studies, etc. Along with these we must also teach how to work together in groups. We must teach how to play and how to problem solve whether it is a math problem or one concerning human relationships. The thinking process and rationality must extend beyond how to solve a math problem or interpret a poem. We must undertake the teaching of cognitive skills that address the underlying dynamics of interpersonal and social issues such as scapegoating and prejudice. We must employ imaginative and creative approaches to learning. We must make it an exciting adventure. We must instill a life long love of learning.

Back to teachers. First of all we must attract qualified people. We must have those who know the subject matter and how to teach it. We must have people who love teaching and who are dedicated to the general well being of children. We have to inspire people to go to college and major in the teaching profession. The colleges must train them adequately.

In order to recruit the right kind of teacher and hold on to them, we must elevate the level of respect we give them. One significant way to do so is to pay them appropriately. Another is to value the schools to such a degree that we fund them adequately. Children should spend their school hours in livable buildings and a healthful environment. They should have the learning materials they need. The teacher-pupil ratio should be reasonable. The teacher should be relieved of many of the non-teaching duties such as lunch room monitoring, policing hallways, and overseeing the unloading and boarding of school buses. They should have administrative responsibilities streamlined so that they have more time to devote to direct child contact. They should be given qualified assistants in the classroom. They need genuine, competent supervision and available qualified consultants. They need continuing educational opportunities.

The content of this book deals with stupidity where it shouldn't be found—among intelligent people. At the societal level, it would be difficult to find a greater degree of stupidity than how we run our schools.

Exploit Advantages of the Computer Age

The term computer age includes the broad spectrum of the technology made possible by the microchip and whatever future evolution that might improve upon it. Included would be the computer, the Internet, the cell phone, video phones, virtual reality, robotics, and so on. The power of this technology embraces the potential of near instant world-wide communication. It includes the capacity for storing and accessing vast amounts of information. It permits complex organizing, systematizing, and analyzing ideas and facts. It can develop hypothetical scenarios and practically look into the future statistically and visually. It can do complex mathematical computations in minutes that would otherwise take a millennium. It can practically duplicate actual experiences with respect to our senses by means of virtual reality devices. One can learn to fly airplanes or master the technique of a complex surgical operation utilizing a simulator. There seems to be no end to the listing of actual applications of the new technology.

When I was a college undergraduate studying sociology in the early 1950's, one of my professors spoke of the knowledge gap. What this phrase addressed was the new knowledge available to us and our inability to put that knowledge to use in a timely manner. I believe there was some speculation about how much time stood between invention/discovery and implementation. If memory serves me well, I believe I heard the figure of ten years. I'm now astounded at such naivete. We haven't even done well in practicing the wisdom of the ages.

I have heard remarks over the past ten or twenty years about how fast knowledge is expanding. There were times when it was said to be doubling every ten years, then three years, and so on. Now, I believe some estimate it to be every six months. If this is so, how can we humans narrow the knowledge gap that surely exists?

The problem with this gap is not just whether or not we can effectively apply this new information in a technical and practical way. The problem is one of determining long range effects. What impact might there be on the human condition in six months, six years, or a hundred years? What impact will it have on the children of this generation? What will their adulthood be like as a consequence? What about later generations? I don't think we know. Do we care? Isn't it easier to just rush on and not ask questions and pursue what would likely be challenging answers?

Perhaps we have now reached the stage in our evolution (or our technical revolution) where we can apply the new technology to answer these tremendous, perplexing questions. Advances in the electronic industry in and of itself is not enough. It is necessary for a great number of wise and capable human beings to take these tools and apply them to the assessment of where our technology is leading us. Along the way, they might help us to put the new knowledge to good use.

Maintain a Program of Personal Growth

A Jungian analyst[102] employed the myth of Parsifal and the Golden Grail to illustrate the life journey of the typical male. There were two times in one's life, he said, when man has the best opportunity to achieve wisdom and harmony. Those times were adolescence and middle age. Few were successful during their adolescence. More than a few succeeded during their middle age. The fact of the matter is—and Jung himself would have agreed—the search for personal fulfillment never ends. There can be rewards of joy along the way but the journey is never complete. The goal is not personal achievement. The goal is not perfection. The goal is wholeness.

Are we intelligent human beings going to minimize the making of stupid mistakes? Are we going to realize our potential before it's too late for us individually and for humankind collectively? If we decide to do so, we must dig deeply within ourselves for answers.

There are many and varied problems in the world. There are natural disasters and the potential for many more. We can develop ways to predict some, fend off some, and to ameliorate the effects of others. There are great problems of our own making. Some of these impact our natural environment. Some have to do with our relating to our fellow human beings. Many of the preceding chapters have identified human-type problems. They touched upon issues having to do with lack of self-control. They included problems concerning dysfunctional marriages, prejudice, violence, political chicanery, and ideological madness to name a few. Understanding these issues and devising practical strategies for their resolution will go only so far. At the core is the need for personal maturity, a maturity that doesn't come by a simple passing of years. Practically every individual has the capacity for improving his psychological well-being. It lies within one's personhood to do so. Along with the development of technology, we have had a growth in knowledge and understanding of the

---

[102] Johnson, Robert A. He: Revised Edition (New York: Harper & Row, 1989).

human psyche. Many promising paths have been laid out that can lead us to harmonious living. Let's hope that we can affirm life and find wholeness by way of one or more of these paths.

CHAPTER *VIII*

Conclusions

The experience of preparing for and writing this book has been something like an intellectual journey. Although, as I mention in the introduction, it represents nearly a lifetime of personal reflection, I had never before tried to approach the topic in a systematic way. I had written nothing before pertaining to the subject. What I soon discovered was that a single volume was insufficient to include a thorough coverage of all the sub-topics.

What this book offers is a comprehensive overview of the vast range of issues having to do with *Why Smart People Do Stupid Things*. Most if not all of the cited sources are deserving of attention from the reader.

Much that went into the preparation deeply saddened me. I found myself at times on the edge of a depressive mood. Obviously, one can't dwell for long on such things as the Holocaust and not have bad feelings. I was surprised how disturbing it was for me to research Richard Nixon, Bill Clinton, and the militia and fundamentalist alliance. These touched upon events too contemporary and too ominous for our present and future.

In 1996 while on a vacation to the Southwest, I took advantage of the opportunity to visit the site of the devastated Alfred P. Murrah Federal Building in downtown Oklahoma City. I was there on April 19th one year to the day from the bombing. The fence holding various memorials still stood. Teddy bears for the children, photographs, poignant letters, etc. abounded. I would soon be at a loss for words if I tried to describe the emotion felt when looking at the vast destruction and when reading notes addressed to the victims by friends and relatives. The force of the explosion was so great as to damage buildings four or five city blocks away. This happened because of two or more very disturbed young men. They were acting out the ideological hatred espoused by hundreds if not thousands of deeply troubled individuals. Among these individuals were intelligent people driven by irrational motives and thoughts. They contributed to the ultimate stupidity—which was the Oklahoma City bombing.

I found in the treatment of the subject matter that there was a progression of concepts from the particular to the general and from the concrete to the abstract. Though I perceive this, the book is only loosely organized according to these schemes. I felt that as a matter of importance the broader conceptual aspects are the most important.

I can substantiate this view by using William Jefferson Clinton as an example. I voted for Clinton as president on the two occasions that he ran for office. The fact was I voted for one party platform and against others that were in contention. I believe the Clinton presidency brought much good to the country. I also believe it introduced what could be called a neuroticism to the American psyche. It takes the form of diminishing the ethical and moral standards we set for our political leaders. I fear this will have a filter-down effect on all of our citizens.

However, it is my opinion that the former President can do what he said he was going to do. With respect to his sexual indiscretions, he has stated publically that he would no longer engage in such behavior. How might he accomplish this goal? How might he fail?

Let's look at the road to failure first. In these types of situations it is possible for a man to see himself as a victim of sorts. It was as much the woman's fault as his he might believe. It could be perceived as a victimless activity. It could be regarded as a personal matter, no one else's business but his own. He might believe that his wife actually condones the behavior. He might have the idea that he works so hard and he has such burdensome responsibilities that he deserves to have some "recreation."

If the sexual behavior is seen only as habituation or addiction, the road to reform can be fraught with difficulty. Imagine equating dependence on smoking, alcohol consumption, and gambling with sexual activity. A closer analogy for sex is with over-eating. The act of eating food is driven by a basic biological need. You must eat or die. That is not so with substance abuse. Engaging in sexual activity is also based upon a basic biological need. Granted one won't die from abstaining from sex, but the biological urge is always lurking in the shadows if not in the forefront of consciousness. Such an urge is compelling. You can refuse to buy cigarettes, avoid going to bars, and stay away from the race track but you will have considerable difficulty not seeing women. They represent over half the population.If the ex-president conceptualizes his difficulty as a moral failure solely or primarily—a violation of his religious principals—then he is in for trouble. Under these circumstances the traditional faith response is to confess in complete humility, pray for forgiveness, and vow to reform. Doing so feels like offering penance, gaining forgiveness, and being given new freedom. The trouble is that this is too formulaic. It doesn't reflect concrete steps that would lead to change. It could very well be without substance and without commitment. So many things in life are easy to affirm but hard to act upon. Dependence on this approach is also like laying the responsibility on God. "Lean on God and I'll get by." The other side of this is "the Devil made me do it."

Let's now look at how Bill Clinton stands a better chance of accomplishing his objective. First, he has to undergird the foundation of his motivation. What does he really want for himself? Why does he want what? We assume he wants to be strictly monogamous in his marriage as he has implied. He would do well to list all the benefits of remaining true to his wife. He should also list all the disadvantages in not doing so. He should get these thoughts firmly implanted in his mind and keep them there. Second, he has to throw away all his rationalizations supporting

198 • *Why Smart People Do Stupid Things*

having sexual encounters with women other than his wife. Thirdly, he needs to look within himself. He needs to attend to the abstract, to the tough issues.

This is where it really counts. He must go into the region of the elusive, nebulous psyche—his own. He has to become acquainted with his dark side. The word "dark" in this context doesn't mean evil. It means hidden. It is like the back side of the moon which we only see if we orbit it in a space module. This region of Bill's mind is also regarded as the unconscious. There are various aspects of his mental functioning which he doesn't know. Not knowing them means that they impact his everyday functioning outside the control of his rational mind.

Bill Clinton, as does everyone, had to define himself with respect to his public image. Though not conscious, it was required of him to be a special sort of person in the eyes of those he encountered in the world. One such very significant person was his mother, Virginia Kelley. Significant also were his maternal grandparents who were his surrogate parents during the first three years of his life. It went on from there with his exposure to a particular aunt, church leaders, teachers, neighbors, and, of course, his peers. His reprobate step-father played a significant role in setting a model of how not to be but also a model of how one might become. Such can give rise to considerable anxiety. His step-father's negative public image over-determined the importance that Bill gave to the way other people regarded him. Only Bill himself, perhaps with the help of a competent psychotherapist, can sort out the unconscious drives that have shaped his persona.

It is so generally accepted that it has become commonplace to think of maleness and femaleness being contained within the personalities of both genders. We speak of one's male side and one's female side. The virile Phil Jackson, coach of the Los Angeles NBA basketball team and former Chicago Bulls coach, seriously speaks about his using his feminine side as a means of relating to his players. Jackson had in mind certain traits that are characteristically and nearly universally attributed to femaleness. A great many men are so uncomfortable with their feminine personality features that they vigorously repress them. Jackson doesn't and he can consciously use them to his advantage. Bill Clinton, on the other hand, isn't in touch with the feminine determinants within his psyche. This is obvious because of the disturbing effects they have on at least two aspects of his relationships with women. One is the over-determination of his being responsible for others—his need to do all for all people. He has been altogether too nurturing on a personal level and on the diplomatic scene. The other is how he relates to women with respect to sexuality.

It would be highly speculative and therefore unproductive to assert how Clinton's repressed feminine side has led him into a pattern of seduction and sexual gratification with various women. The responsibility for ferreting out his unconscious drives must remain with him. However, the sorts of things men may do when they fail to properly integrate their innate femaleness includes the following. The women they choose to marry would share prominent traits with the mother, traits the man finds fulfilling. A possible consequence of this would be to create a barrier between the husband's and wife's sexual relationship. It could establish a "Madonna complex," where the wife is regarded as pure and sexless. Allied to this would be the classical Oedipal situation where the wife's image is too closely associated with the mother. Examples of shared traits might include strength of character and dedication to loved ones.

Citing another example where the male's repressed feminine side might lead him is to seek out women who are manifestly feminine in their personality. They are very likely to present themselves in a seductive manner, appear helpless, and seem unassertive. They might appear to be signaling a desire to be taken care of by a man.

Men must deal with other men during their lives. All that goes into shaping the behaviors of a man in relating to other men is not conscious. Some of the these unconscious determinants are rooted in a child's relationship with his father or other significant males who play a part during the formative years of a man's life. (Such influence is sometimes referred to as role models good or bad. However, the modeling is very often at an unconscious level. It is not always like the little boy looking up in admiration at the idealized, heroic athlete). An example of how a child might adopt traits from an adult male includes the unreliability and deceitfulness of an alcoholic father-figure. Another example would be absorbing the gregariousness of a lovable grandfather. The unconscious male paradigm for behavior has much to do with how a man expresses his aggressivity. The more in touch he is with that inner maleness the more likely his aggressiveness would be conscious and adaptive.

What we look for for ourselves, for others, and particularly for our leaders is what we might loosely call maturity. Most would say that integrity of character would be a part of this. Such character means adherence to moral standards and honesty. Integrity also means the state of being whole and undiminished.

To value wholeness within a person implies that there are various parts that together define the person. To attain wholeness, it is necessary to identify these various parts, become acquainted with them, and to see how they fit the total picture—the personality picture. Students and scientists of human behavior have hypothesized a variety of parts that form man's mind. Perhaps chief among these parts, ones that have gained the widest acceptance, are the conscious and unconscious. As the thinking goes, one has rational control over that which is conscious. He doesn't over the unconscious. That which is unconscious, nevertheless, exerts power over how we think and act. Behaviors unconsciously driven are not necessarily evil or destructive. However, because there is a lack of conscious control, the ever active unconscious typically causes trouble. To achieve the desired wholeness we seek, we must integrate these components.

A word having some currency is that of "authenticity." This has meant, in general, one who is true to himself, who is genuine. There is a presumption that each person has a core of being which is basically good. Let's hope that all the elements of our personhood can be assembled around that core of being and reflect its great worth.

Why Smart People Do Stupid Things documents a formidable truism. It is one we rarely confront in a conscious and determined way. It is the fact that as a species—as civilized beings—we are continually walking on the edge of disasters of our own making. Our animal nature has suffered in the process of our becoming civilized. Man's animal-like basic instincts remain a part of who we are now. However, that part has become twisted in such a way that it is often our enemy rather than the friend it should be.

The civilizing process too often emerged by denying our basic nature. Denial wasn't the appropriate path. Rather, it was required that we accommodate and integrate our animal selves into our full personhood. We have generally failed in this task. We must devote ourselves to rethinking and to devising ways toward making profound changes in how we conduct our lives individually and especially collectively.

Bibliography

Adorno, T. W. *et al. The Authoritarian Personality* (New York: Harper Brothers, 1950).

Allport, Gordon. *The Nature of Prejudice* (New York: Doubleday & Company, Inc., 1954).

Berlet, Chip and Lyons Matthew N. *Right Wing Populism in America: Too Close for Comfort* (New York: the Guilford Press, 2000).

Boston, Robert. *Close Encounters with the Religious Right* (New York: Prometheus Books, 2000).

Breisach, Ernst. *Introduction to Modern Existentialism* (New York: Grove Press, Inc. 1962).

Brill, A. A. [Ed.] *The Basic Writings of Sigmund Freud.* (New York: Random House, Inc., 1938).

Buber, Martin [Trans. by Kaufmann, Walter] *I and Thou* (New York: Charles Scribner's Sons, 1970).

Carnes, Patrick. *The Sexual Addiction* (Minneapolis: CompCare Publications, 1983).

Collins, Joseph. *Adult Infantilism in the United States* [or prefaced by: *A Doctor Looks at*] (Publisher unknown, copywrite circa. 1930).

Coppola, Vincent. *Dragon's of God: A Journey Through Far-Right America* (Marietta, Georgia: Longstreet Press, Inc., 1996).

Dabbs, James McBride and Dabbs, Mary Godwin. *Hereos Rogues and Lovers: Testosterone and Behavior* (New York: McGraw-Hill, 2000).

Dees, Morris with Corcoran, James. *Gathering Storm: America's Militia Threat* (New York: HarperCollings Publisher, 1996).

Evans, Ivor H. *Brewer's Dictionary of Phrase and Fable* (New York: Harper & Rowe,).

Fick, Paul. *The Dysfunctional President: Understanding the Compulsions of Bill Clinton* (Secaucus, NJ: Carol Publishing Group, 1998).

Fierman, Louis B. *Effective Psychotherapy: the Contribution of Hellmuth Kaiser* (New York: Collier-Macmillan Limited, London, 1965).

Frankfurt, Harry G. "Freedom of the Will and the Concept of a Person." In Rosenthal, David M. *The Nature of Mind* (New York: Oxford University Press, 1991).

Freud, Sigmund. "Psychology of Everyday Life" as contained in Brill, A. A. [Ed.] *The Basic Writings of Sigmund Freud* (New York: The Modern Library, 1938).

Gardner, Howard. *Frames of Mind: The Theory of Multiple Intelligences* (New York: Basic Books, 1983).

Gardner, Howard. *Intelligence Reframed: Multiple Intelligences for the 21st Century* (New York: Basic Books, 1999).

Goleman, Daniel. *Emotional Intelligence: Why It Can Matter More Than IQ* (New York: Bantam Books, 1995).

Guilford, J. P. *The Nature of Human Intelligence* (New York: McGraw-Hill Book Company, 1967).

Hinds, William Alfred. *American Communities* (New York: Corinth Books, Inc. 1961 [reprinted from 1879]).

Hinsie, Leland E. and Campbell, Robert J. *Psychiatric Dictionary* (New York: Oxford University Press, 1970).

Holloway, Mark. *Heavens on Earth: Utopian Communities in America: 1680-1880* (New York: Dover Publications, Inc., 1966).

Jourard, Sidney M. *The Transparent Self* (New York, D. Van Norstrand Company, Inc., 1964).

Johnson, Robert A. *He: Revised Edition* (New York: Harper & Row, 1989).

Johnson, Robert A. *Owning Your Own Shadow: Understanding the Dark Side of the Psyche* (New York: HarperCollins, 1993).

Johnson, Wendell. *People in Quandaries* (New York: Harper & Brothers, 1946).

Kaufmann, Walter. *I and Thou: Martin Buber: A New Translation* (New York: Charles Scribner's Sons, 1970).

Keyes, Kenneth S. Jr. *How to Develop Your Thinking Ability* (New York: McGraw-Hill Book Company, Inc., 1950).

Korzybski, Alfred. *Science and Sanity: An Introduction to Non-Aristotelian Systems and General Semantics* (Lancaster: Science Press, 2nd Edition, 1941).

Lakoff, Robin Tolmach. *The Language War* (Berkeley: University of California Press, 2000).

Lamy, Philip. *Millennium Rage: Survivalists, White Supremacists, and the Doomsday Prophecy* (New York: Plenum Press, 1996).

Lech, Raymond B. *Broken Soldiers* (Chicago: University of Illinois Press, 2000).

Leckie, Robert. *Conflict: The History of the Korean War* (New York: Putnam, 1962).

Matthews, Peter. *The Concise Oxford Dictionary of Linguistics* (New York: Oxford University Press, 1997).

Menninger, Karl. *Whatever Became of Sin?* (New York: Hawthorn Books, Inc., 1973).

Onions, C. T. [Ed.] *The Oxford Dictionary of English Etymology* (New York: Oxford Press, 1966).

Pollack, William S. *Real Boy's Voices* (New York: Random House, 2000).

Raban, Jonathan. *Bad Land: An American Romance* (London, England: Picador, 1997).

Reik, Theodore. *The Search Within: The Inner Experiences of a Psychoanalyst* (New York: Grove Press, Inc., 1956).

Rohrback, Elizabeth C. [Ed.] *Jung's Contribution to Our Time: The Collected Papers of Eleanor Bertine* (New York: G. P. Putnam's Sons, 1967).

Rokeach, Milton. *The Open and Closed Mind* (New York: Basic Books, Inc. 1960).

Snyder, George E. *Don't Be A Spin Sucker* (Lincoln, Nebraska: Writers Club Press, 2000).

Summers, Anthony. *The Arrogance of Power: the Secret World of Richard Nixon* (New York: Viking, 2000).

Starkey, Marion L. *The Devil in Massachusetts* (New York: Doubleday & Company, Inc., Anchor Books Edition, 1969).

Thouless, Robert H. *How to Think Straight* (New York: Hart Publishing Company, Inc.,1932).

Tillich, Paul. *Love, Power, and Justice* (New York: Oxford University Press, 1954).

Toobin, Jeffrey. *A Vast Conspiracy: The Real Story of the Sex Scandal that Nearly Brought Down a President* (New York: Touchstone, 1999).

Van Wesep, H. B. *Seven Sages: The Story of American Philosophy* (New York: Longmans, Green and Co., 1960).

Weatherford, Roy C. "Freedom and Determinism" in *The Oxford Companion to Philosophy* [Ed. By Honderich, Ted] (New York: Oxford University Press, 1995).

White, Robert W. *The Abnormal Personality: A Textbook* (New York: The Ronald Press Company, 1956).

Index